THE JUICER BOOK

Joanna White

Bristol Publishing Enterprises, Inc.
San Leandro, California

A Nitty Gritty® Cookbook

Printed in the United States of America.

ISBN 1-55867-040-8

Cover design: Frank Paredes
Front cover photography: John Benson
Food stylist: Stephanie Greenleigh
Back cover photography: Shel Izen
Illustrator: James Balkovek

CONTENTS

Dedicated to my family and friends who have
always encouraged and supported
my interest in the culinary field and nutrition.

INFORMATION ABOUT JUICE AND JUICERS

Finally, nutrition is beginning to get national recognition! People are beginning to recognize that the "American Diet" is not healthy. Cooking, processing and preserving destroys much of the nutritional value of food. We need to feed "live" fresh food to our bodies in its natural state so we can utilize all the nutrients.

A healthier life style is becoming the way of the future and juicing is one of the best ways to start making the transition to healthier living. Juicers can separate the nutrients from the fiber even more efficiently than your own digestive system, so you can receive the maximum nutritional food value. You would have to consume very large quantities of produce to get the equivalent nutritional value from the juice (for example, 1 cup of carrot juice contains the equivalent nutrition of 4 cups of raw carrots). But remember that it is still important to eat fresh fruits and vegetables daily because fiber is a necessary part of a balanced diet, to ensure a healthy gastrointestinal tract and to help prevent some forms of heart disease and cancer.

The recipes in this book show you how to juice most of basic fruits and vegetables and how to use the fresh juices in recipes to enhance the flavor and nutrition. Also included are recipes that utilize the fruit and vegetable pulp so you can take advantage of the natural fiber and add some additional flavor, as well as avoid wasting the residue.

It is important to take a few minutes to go through the section, *Do's and Don'ts of Juicing*, page 9, before you begin. Crucial points like not mixing fruit and vegetable juices together can save you possible stomach distress. Everyone I have introduced to juicing can't get over how wonderful fresh juices taste and how much more energetic they feel. Juicers are well worth the investment — so juice and enjoy!

ADVANTAGES OF JUICING

- If juices are made fresh and are consumed right on the spot, the juices instantly release nourishment to the bloodstream. Therefore, the body does not need to expend excessive amounts of energy on digestion.

- Juices are made very quickly with little clean-up needed, which fits well into our now fast-moving lifestyle.

- A masticating juicer can utilize the whole fruit or vegetable including the peels, seeds, rinds, and stems so that you can receive maximum food value. Bottled juices are processed, sterilized and sometimes "preserved" so that most of the nutritional value is destroyed.

- Our digestive process is less efficient at separating the nutritious juice from the fiber and as we age this process becomes even less efficient. Because of this we can absorb as little as 10% of the nutritional value of the food, but juicing can supply up to 95% of the nutrients.

- Fresh-made juices have a delightful, intense flavor that you can't get from bottled juices. Also juicing provides a wonderful way to use up excessive produce.

CHOOSING A JUICER

BLENDERS

A blender cannot produce a proper juice because it does not break down the fiber and separate it from the liquid. The only possible way of using a blender to produce juice would be to puree the fruit or vegetable into a mush with water, and then squeeze the puree through a fine mesh cloth. This is very time-consuming and inefficient. Blenders are best used to liquify soft fruits like bananas, or low-fiber fruits like watermelon, or simply for mixing ingredients together. They do not remove pulp.

CITRUS JUICERS

This refers to the old-fashioned cone-shaped juicer in which you press the halved fruit down on a cone, and extract a juice that filters through holes, leaving behind seeds. Such juicers are all manually controlled: you either apply the pressure and turn the fruit, or the cone, powered by a motor, spins and you press the fruit down on it. The problem with this type of juicer is that you are restricted to a few fruits only, and without the masticating blades to break down the fibers you are missing much of the nutrition.

MASTICATING JUICERS

Masticating means that there are blades which tear the fibers apart, producing a fine paste which is then squeezed through a screen. This produces a very fine (pulp-free) juice. The Champion is probably the best known of this type of juicer. It has the added features of allowing you to change the screens to homogenize foods (excellent for baby foods) or to remove the screen to finely grate the produce. It has the capability of grinding seeds, nuts, sprouted grains and dried fruits which no other juicer (that I know of) can do. It also can blend frozen fruit for ice creams and frozen desserts. The residue pulp is soft and on the moist side.

MASTICATING JUICER WITH HYDRAULIC PRESS

This is a high-speed juicer that masticates the fruit or vegetables into a paste, automatically squeezing it into a cotton bag, and then hydraulically presses it. The Norwalk brand is the best known of this type, it produces a high quality juice, but it is very expensive. Because of their size and weight, these juicers are often used in institutional kitchens.

CENTRIFUGAL JUICERS

The centrifugal juicer is a high-speed juicer that masticates the fruits or vegetables and then spins at high speed to separate the juice from the pulp. Some juicers have a basket in which the pulp remains until it is removed. There are filter papers available which fit inside the basket for ease in removing the pulp and cleaning.

Other centrifugal juicers have a pulp ejector which automatically ejects the pulp through a side opening. The advantage of centrifugal juicers is that you get the best yield of juice from the produce because of the extra spinning action. The juice has a tendency to contain a little more pulp and not be quite as fine as the masticating (noncentrifugal) juicers. The pulp (or residue) from the centrifugal juicer is very dry and some liquid may need to be added to recipes using this pulp.

Popular centrifugal juicers include Acme, Juiceman, Olympic, Phoenix, Braun, Oster, Sanyo, Panasonic, Sony and Salton.

BUYING, CLEANING AND STORING PRODUCE

General rules for choosing produce:

- Try to buy organically grown produce if possible (especially carrots). If organically grown produce is not available, be sure to use the formula for removing toxic sprays from non-organically grown produce listed below.

- Select fresh, plump, smooth, and unblemished produce whenever possible.

- When buying fruit, you can smell ripeness. Avoid hard green fruits and watch for overripe fruits that take on a musky odor.

Formula and method for removing toxic surface sprays from non-organic produce:

1. Fill sink with cold water.
2. Add 4 tablespoons of salt and 1 tablespoon of fresh lemon juice.
3. Soak fruits and vegetables for 10 minutes.
4. Soak leafy greens for approximately 3 minutes.
5. Soak berries for 2 minutes. (Berries are best if washed just before using).
6. Rinse everything in cold water after soaking.

Storage of produce:

- Spin dry leafy greens after washing and store in plastic bags.

- Vegetables which are stored in the refrigerator either in a crisper or plastic bag: artichokes, asparagus, beans, beets, bok choy, broccoli, Brussels sprouts, cabbage, carrots, cauliflower, celery, celery root, chard, corn, cucumber, eggplant, green onions, Jerusalem artichokes, jicama, kohlrabi, leeks, mushrooms, okra, parsley, parsnips, peas, peppers, radishes, rutabagas, sprouts, summer squash, turnips, and zucchini.

- Vegetables best stored at room temperature: avocado, garlic, onions, potatoes, pumpkins, shallots, tomatoes, winter squash.

- Fruits are best stored at room temperature so they can continue to ripen. (Refrigerate to slow ripening).

Storage of fresh juice:

Generally, fresh juice should be consumed immediately after juicing because it begins to immediately oxidize and lose its potency. But if you need to store it, the best method is to place a stainless steel thermos in the freezer overnight; in the morning fill the fresh juice to the top and screw on the lid (making sure there is no air left in the thermos). Keeping it air-tight and cold should keep the juice fresh for several hours.

DO'S AND DON'TS OF JUICING

General Tips

- Feed produce slowly into the juicer without using force.

- Put carrots in large end first.

- Bunch greens up in clumps and tap them through with a pusher or carrot.

- Soft fruits such as bananas, apricots, figs, etc., are not suitable for juicing because a clear juice cannot be obtained and residue left in the machine could damage the motor.

- Pears can be used if firm (juice them with apples, alternating the apple and pear pieces, always starting and ending with an apple piece).

- Do not combine fruits and vegetables together because their enzymes are not compatible with the exception of apples (use an apple to clean out the juicer when switching between fruit and vegetable drinks).

- Do not drink greens or beets alone; they should be mixed with carrots (use 3 parts carrot to one part greens or beets).

- Leave peelings, seeds and stems on all fruits and vegetables with the exception of oranges and grapefruits (you should remove the colored peel, but leave the pithy white part).

- It is best not to mix melons with other fruits (they require different enzymes to digest).

- Wait between drinking juices:

  fruit - wait 1 minute before drinking vegetable juices.
  vegetable - wait 10 minutes before drinking fruit juices.

HEALING PROPERTIES OF JUICES

APPLES
Gall bladder troubles, liver, diarrhea, tooth decay, and loss of appetite.

APRICOTS
Detoxifies the liver and pancreas.

ASPARAGUS
Helps with urinary problems and fatty tumors.

BEETS
Spleen food. Also an alkalizer, good for nerves and anemia.

BELL PEPPER
Good for eyes and digestion.

BLACKBERRY
Good for diarrhea and colon problems.

BLUEBERRY
Feeds the pancreas and good for sugar problems.

CABBAGE
For vitamin C, tissue builder, removes toxins, helps digestion and elimination.

CANTALOUPE
For complexion and digestion.

CARROTS
For eyes, blood, lymph, skin and digestion.

CELERY
A reducing aid, good for arthritis, heart, indigestion, colds and skin problems.

CHERRIES
For gout and as a blood cleanser.

CRAB APPLE
For vertigo.

CRANBERRY
Good for kidneys and asthma.

CUCUMBER	Good as a skin remedy, bladder and kidney cleanser, for infection and nerves.
GRAPEFRUIT	A lime supplier, good for malaria, laxative, colds, flu, and sleeplessness.
GRAPES	Good for anemia and tumors.
GREEN BEANS	Removes metallic poison and good for malfunctions of the pancreas.
KALE	For resistance to colds.
LEEK	For reducing, pancreas problems and as a tissue builder.
LEMON	High in vitamin C and bioflavenoids. Good for nerves, kidneys, high blood pressure, rheumatism and arthritis.
LETTUCE	Aids digestion, kidneys, lung, nerves. High in iron.
LIME	For yellow jaundice and supplier of vitamin C.
ONION	Good for colds and flu.
ORANGES	High vitamin C and good for flu.
PAPAYA	For protein digestion.
PARSNIP	For intolerance to milk.
PARSLEY	Laxative, detoxicant, good for piles, gall stones, gas, elimination and anemia. Also a great diuretic.
PEACHES	Good during pregnancy.

PEAS	Good source of protein and good for weak stomachs.
PEARS	Strengthens kidney and colon, also good for sleeplessness.
PINEAPPLE	Excellent enzyme supplier and helps digest protein.
POTATOES	For kidney ailments (must include the peeling).
RADISHES	Promotes bile flow.
ROMAINE	For asthma and bronchitis.
RHUBARB	Colon cleanser.
SPINACH	Alkalizer, good for anemia, constipation, and chronic infections.
STRAWBERRY	A skin berry, high in vitamin C.
TOMATO	Infections, liver, kidney, anemia, and high in vitamin C.
TURNIPS	For tumors.
WATERCRESS	High in vitamin C and E, alkalizer, good for anemia, rheumatism and infections.
WATERMELON	Wonderful for kidneys, a natural diuretic. Also good for the lungs (best if you include the rind).

HEALING PROPERTIES OF COMBINATION JUICES

APPLES-OKRA ulcers
APPLE-CELERY headaches
BLUEBERRY-BANANA pancreatitis
CARROT-APPLE cancer (take up to 13 glasses per day)
CARROT-CABBAGE cleanses mucous from the stomach and good for pyorrhea
CARROT-CELERY-CABBAGE ulcers
CARROT-CUCUMBER-BEET gall bladder, liver, kidneys and prostate
CARROT-LETTUCE-SPINACH stimulates hair growth
CABBAGE-CELERY-CARROT-SPINACH-APPLE hangovers and high in
    calcium
GRAPEFRUIT-PINEAPPLE arthritis
PEAR-APPLE sleeplessness

GENERAL INFORMATION ABOUT BABY FOOD

Natural baby foods are so easy, nutritious and flavorful that you will probably never go back to the store for baby food.

FRUIT JUICES

- Any fruit juice is good but should be diluted one-half with water because it is so concentrated.

HOMOGENIZED FRUIT

- If you have a blank screen attachment, simply remove the seeds and stems and process through the grating disk.

- Another alternative is to remove the seeds, stems and rinds (if using oranges or grapefruits), and juice. Then mix the pulp and the juice together. If the pulp is too coarse then simply run the pulp through the feed tube again.

VEGETABLE JUICES

- Use any vegetable juice diluted one-half with water. But be very careful not to use too many greens or beets without mixing with ⅔ carrot juice; otherwise the mixture may be too potent for young stomachs.

- Sweeten vegetable juices with apples to make more palatable for babies (remember — apples are the only fruit which should be mixed with vegetables).

HOMOGENIZED VEGETABLES

- If you have a blank screen attachment, simply remove any seeds, stems, or very tough skins and process through the grating disk. Otherwise, simply mix the pulp and juice together.

DRINKS AND PUNCHES

INCREDIBLE LEMONADE

Servings: 1

Such a simple combination, but the best all-natural lemonade I have ever had!

4 large apples (I prefer Golden
Delicious)

½ lemon (peel included)

Cut up apples (leaving peel, stem and seeds) and push into juicer. Add lemon including peel and push into juicer. Sample and adjust to your personal taste by adding either more apple or lemon for sweetness or tartness.

VITAMIN HIGH

Servings: 1

This particular combination of fruits is extremely high in vitamins A, B1, B2, and C and tastes good too!

1 peach, pitted
1 apple

½ cup fresh grape juice

Juice peach (skin and all). Then juice apple (skin, peel and stem). Lastly juice enough grapes (skin, seeds and stems) to produce ½ cup of juice. Depending on sweetness of grapes and the variety used you may need to increase apple to adjust the sweetness.

FRUITY YOGURT SMOOTHY

This is one of my favorite breakfast drinks. By varying the combination of fruits and the yogurt flavors the choices are endless.

2 cups fresh fruit juice (orange, pineapple, strawberry, blueberry, raspberry, apple, peach, pear, watermelon, cantaloupe, or a combination)
1 cup nonfat or lowfat yogurt (plain or flavored)
½ cup crushed ice or ½ frozen banana
flavored extracts or sweeteners to taste, optional

Combine all ingredients in a blender or food processor and blend until smooth.

NOTE: If you have bananas getting too ripe for eating, peel, cut into 1-inch pieces and freeze in ziploc bags.

MELON MADNESS

Servings: 2

Melons are full of vitamins and nutrients and are a tremendous energy booster. The rind of the watermelon contains so much of the nutrients that I would highly recommend using it.

1 cup cantaloupe juice (skin included)
1 cup honeydew melon juice
1 cup watermelon juice (rind included)

Cut cantaloupe up (including skin and seeds) and juice. You can include honeydew skin, but it may cut down quite a bit on sweetness. Next juice watermelon (including skin and seeds).

QUIET TIME FRUITS

Servings: 1

This is one of my favorite drinks in the evening. The combination is delicious and acts like a natural sedative.

1 peach, pitted   1 apple
1 pear (on the hard side)

Juice peach (skin included). Juice pear (stem and skin included) alternating pieces with apple (skin and seeds) so the softer pear doesn't clog the machine.

GINGER APPLE DRINK

Servings: 1

Ginger is a spicy way to treat apple juice and also has a great side effect of sweetening the breath.

1 piece fresh ginger root (approximately ½-inch long)

3 apples (peel, seeds and stem)

Cut ginger root into small pieces and feed alternately into juicer with apple pieces.

BLUEBERRY SNACK

Servings: 1

Blueberries are extremely high in vitamin C and low in sugar, but naturally sweet, which makes them ideal for a "snack" drink. Pears are mildly diuretic and have a somewhat laxative effect.

½ cup blueberries

2 pears, hard variety

Juice blueberries and pears (skin, stem and seeds included).

TROPICAL CREAM

This combination is great in the summer, but consider making it in the dead of winter (with frozen strawberries) to remind you of the tropics! Strawberries are very high in vitamin C.

1 cup fresh pineapple juice
¾ cup strawberry juice
½ cup crushed ice

½ cup plain yogurt, cream, or
  even ice cream
½ cup coconut cream

If not using pulp, juice pineapple with rind. Juice either fresh or frozen straw-berries. Combine remaining ingredients in a food processor or blender and adjust sweetness to personal taste.

NOTE: Coconut creams vary in thickness, sweetness and flavor — so don't be afraid to experiment.

CREAMY ORANGE

You can do so many things with orange juice because it is such a popular flavor. Oranges are high in vitamin C and minerals.

1½ cups fresh orange juice
¼ cup honey, optional
1 cup milk or plain yogurt
½ tsp. vanilla
¾ cup crushed ice

Juice oranges with pith (but not peel). Add remaining ingredients in a blender or food processor and adjust sweetness to your personal taste.

NOTE: Consider changing the flavor of the yogurt for variety or even substituting ice cream!

BERRY GOOD

Servings: 2

There are endless combinations you can use with berries. My personal favorite is raspberry, which is so good and the juicer removes the seeds!

2 cups fresh raspberry juice
2 tbs. fresh lemon juice

2 cups fresh apple juice
sugar or honey to taste

Combine all ingredients in a blender or food processor, taste and adjust to your personal sweetness.

NOTE: You can use fresh or frozen raspberries (but remember the frozen need quite a bit more sweetener).

CITROBERRY

Servings: 1

Strawberries contain natural pain killers, are rich in vitamin C and minerals and are highly cleansing to the blood. All this and good taste too!

3 cups fresh strawberry juice
2 tbs. fresh lemon or lime juice

2 cups fresh orange juice

Mix juices in a blender or food processor. Depending on tartness of berries, you may need to add a sweetener.

SPARKLING PEACH

Servings: 4

Fresh peach juice is rich in vitamin A, B-1, B-2, C, niacin and minerals. It cleanses the intestines and has been known to help with morning sickness. Because it is naturally a thick juice, it needs to be thinned down with another liquid.

2 cups fresh peach juice
3 cups sparkling water, sparkling wine, or wine cooler

Remove pits and juice ripe peaches (with skins on). Pour peach juice into a glass and add sparkling liquid. The proportions of juice to sparkling liquid can vary according to personal taste.

MANGO MAGIC

Servings: 4

Mangos have finally become a regular item at the markets. The flavor is exotic and delicious.

4 mangos
1 lemon or lime

4 cups sparkling water
1 cup crushed ice

Remove pits from mangos and juice (with peel). Then juice lemon (or lime) with peel. Pour all ingredients into a blender or food processor and process until mixed.

BANANA FRAPPÉ

Servings: 4

This is excellent as a starter drink for a party with a tropical theme. Only problem is that they might not want dinner!

½ cup fresh pineapple juice
4 bananas, mashed
4 eggs
3 oz. brandy
½ cup light rum
½ cup cream
3 tbs. brown sugar
3 oz. sweet and sour mix
2 cups crushed ice

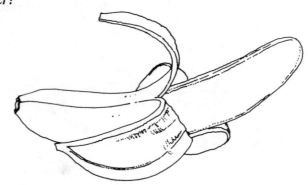

Blend pineapple juice, bananas, eggs, brandy, rum, cream, brown sugar and sweet and sour mix together. Add crushed ice and blend. Serve immediately or keep very chilled until ready to serve.

MORNING TONIC

I can't recommend this enough for people with arthritis or joint problems. Both pineapple and grapefruit have anti-inflammatory properties and are rich in vitamin C.

¼ pineapple
1 grapefruit

Wash pineapple well, discard top leaves and juice with skin on. Peel colored part of grapefruit (but leave on white pith) and juice. Mix together and drink immediately.

NOTE: The pith of the grapefruit contains a tremendous amount of nutrients but sometimes it can be a little bitter. Either increase the pineapple juice or add some apple to sweeten if desired.

WATERMELON COOLER

Servings: 4

Watermelon juice is wonderful cleanser for the kidneys and bladder. I use the rind in juicing because it lowers that sugar content, and dramatically increases the vitamins, minerals and chlorophyll.

3 cups watermelon juice
1 cup frozen lemon yogurt or sherbet
¼ cup fresh raspberry juice
1 cup crushed ice

Juice watermelon (with rinds and seeds). In a food processor or blender, mix watermelon juice, frozen yogurt, raspberry juice and crushed ice together and blend until smooth. Add more frozen yogurt if you want it sweeter.

STRAWBERRY FRAPPÉ

Servings: 2

There are endless things that you can do with strawberries. They mix well with almost any fruit and add a natural sweetness. Strawberries contain a natural painkiller (called organic salycilates).

1 cup fresh grapefruit or orange juice
½ cup fresh strawberry juice
3 tbs. honey or sugar
½ cup soda or 7-Up
1 cup crushed ice

Remove peel (but not pith) from either grapefruit or orange and juice. Juice strawberries. Mix all ingredients in a blender or food processor until well blended. Taste and adjust flavor to personal sweetness. Serve immediately.

FRESH PEACH MARGARITAS

Servings: 1

Fresh peach margaritas are a delightful way to begin a Mexican meal. Also consider using nectarines as a delicious alternative.

2 cups fresh peach juice
2 tbs. fresh lemon or lime juice
1 cup crushed ice
4 oz. tequila, optional
fresh peach slice or lemon slice for garnish

Juice peaches, removing pit but leaving peeling on. Combine peach juice, lemon (or lime) juice, crushed ice and tequila in a blender or food processor and quickly mix well. Adjust quantity of tequila to your personal taste. Garnish and serve immediately.

NOTE: If you chose to use nectarines you may need to add a little sugar depending on the ripeness of the fruit.

CARRAPPLE

Either by themselves or mixed together, both carrots and apples make a delicious drink that is highly nutritious. Carrots are chock full of vitamins, minerals (especially calcium) and protein. Apples make carrot juice much more palatable for newcomers to the juicing world, on top of adding a lot of good nutrition.

6 carrots (I prefer organically
   grown carrots when available)

2 apples (I like Golden Delicious)

Scrub carrots but leave peels on. Cut about ½-inch off tops and juice, inserting large end in first (this prevents carrot from sticking in juicing tube). Next wash apples, (leave peelings, stem and seeds in), cut into pieces to fit juicing tube, and push through juicer. Mix juices together and drink immediately.

NOTE: If you are planning to use the apple pulp, remove the stem and seeds before juicing but leave the peelings because they contain a lot of vitamins and minerals.

CABBAGE TONIC

Servings: 1

There are whole books just on the curative properties of cabbage. The ancient Greeks used it as a tonic, rejuvenator and "cure for baldness." It's best known for its help with digestive problems, especially ulcers.

¼ head cabbage (green or red)
3 celery stalks (without the leaves)
2 apples

Cut cabbage into wedges to fit the juicing tube, then juice. Cut celery stalks into about 4-inch pieces (discarding the leaves because they impart a bitter flavor), and juice. Next cut apples into pieces (leaving peelings, stem and seeds on) and juice. Mix together and drink immediately.

NOTE: Cabbage juice if taken in large quantities may cause some intestinal cramping and gas — so take in moderation to start with or dilute with water.

32 DRINKS AND PUNCHES

WHEATGRASS HIGH

Wheatgrass is grown from wheat berries and can be bought in flats at many health food stores. It is known for its remarkable regenerative and anti-aging properties.

½ cup wheatgrass
5 carrots, unpeeled
2 apples (without the leaves)
½ cup parsley
2 celery stalks

Wad wheatgrass into a ball and push down the feed tube with carrots (which have about ½-inch cut off tops). Next cut apples into tube-size pieces and juice with peelings. Wad parsley into a ball and push down tube with celery stalks that have been cut into 3-inch to 4-inch pieces. Taste. Add an additional apple if more sweetness is desired.

GREEN ENERGY

Servings: 1

Yes, even lettuce can be juiced! As a general rule: the darker the lettuce, the more the nutritional value. It is an excellent source of calcium, iron and vitamins A and E, and is good for anemia, hair loss and weight loss.

1 cup lettuce leaves
2 celery stalks (without leaves)
1 apple (skin, stem and seeds included)

Wad lettuce leaves into a ball and push into the tube (with a bouncing motion) using celery stalks and apple pieces for pushers. If a sweeter juice is desired, just increase apples.

NOTE: The most nutritious lettuce varieties are romaine, butter, and bibb. Also, celery and apple juice can sometimes help with headache relief.

YOUR OWN V-8 SPECIAL

You can create your own vegetable drink full of vitamins and minerals and vary the ingredients according to your personal taste.

2 carrots, unpeeled
1 cup fresh spinach
½ tomato
¼ cucumber (skin and seed)

1 celery stalk
1 green onion
½ red pepper
½ cup cabbage

Cut about ½ inch off tops of carrots and feed into the machine large end first. Wad spinach into a ball and push into machine with prepared carrots. Slowly feed remaining ingredients (skin, seeds and all) into machine and taste.

NOTE: Carrots will add a natural sweetness to the drink — so increase the carrots for a more pleasant flavor. Apple is also a natural sweetener and is the only fruit that can be mixed with vegetables.

THE TONER

Servings: 1

This specific combination of vegetable juices is wonderful for the skin, very high in vitamin C, and apple makes it sweet so even children can enjoy it.

3 carrots
½ cucumber (I like the English variety)
½ green pepper
½ cup watercress
1 cup spinach leaves
1 apple (or more to taste)

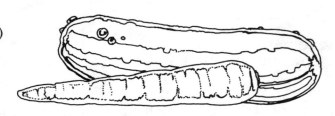

Insert washed (but not peeled) carrot in feed tube, large end first. Juice cucumber (with peel), green pepper, watercress and spinach (wad the leaves into balls and feed down the tube with the pusher, using a tapping motion). Add apple and taste. Increase apple if a sweeter drink is desired. Drink immediately for best benefits.

SPRING TONIC

Servings: 2

High in vitamin A — the addition of the sprouts and carrots makes it high in protein.

1 cup alfalfa sprouts
½ cup asparagus
2 carrots

½ cup kale leaves
1 cup chopped cabbage
1 apple

Feed alfalfa down the tube with a tapping motion. Wash asparagus well and juice. Feed unpeeled carrots down tube, large end first, and finish with cabbage and apple. Taste and add more apple if you like it sweeter.

ENERGY HIGH

Servings: 2

It may seem strange to juice turnips and fennel, but it can give you tremendous energy. Fennel has a slight licorice flavor that surprises people.

2 cups mixed sprouts
1 turnip
3 carrots

½ cup fennel (chopped)
1 apple

Feed sprouts down the tube with a tapping motion. Cut turnip up (leaving the peeling on) and juice. Add carrot (with peel), large end first, and finish with fennel and apple. Taste and add more apple if additional sweetness is desired.

FRESH TOMATO JUICE

Servings: 2

When tomatoes are in season and you have an abundance, consider making fresh tomato juice. Tomatoes (if they have not been cooked, sterilized or processed) are high in calcium, vitamin C and a good for bladder, gall bladder, gout, liver, kidney, skin and weight loss. Tomatoes will yield about 8 to 10 ounces of juice per pound.

2 lb. fresh tomatoes   salt, optional

Leave peeling, stem and seeds intact and simply cut into wedges and juice. Add salt to taste if desired.

TOMATO JUICE COCKTAIL

Servings: 2

3 large tomatoes
½ cucumber
2 celery stalks
Tabasco, optional

optional spices: cayenne, basil, tarragon, dill, nutmeg, ginger or curry
salt and/or pepper to taste

Cut tomatoes into wedges and juice (seeds and peelings). Juice cucumber with peel. Cut celery into 4-inch pieces and feed down the tube (don't force — feed with a steady motion). Some people like to add spices or seasonings for a little spark or even Tabasco.

THE ALKALIZER

Due to the excessive consumption of meats, eggs, sweets, and starches we often become highly acidic. This specific combination of vegetables is great for balancing out that acidity.

10 oz. fresh carrot juice
3 oz. fresh beet juice
3 oz. fresh cucumber juice
2 oz. fresh apple juice

Cut tops off carrots and juice (with the peel), large end first. Scrub beet well, cut into thin wedges and feed down the tube with a tapping motion. Juice cucumber with peel. Cut apple into wedges (including skin, stem and seeds) and push through tube.

NOTE: The apple juice isn't necessary, but I have found when introducing people to vegetable juices that it is more palatable if a little fresh apple juice is added.

NUT OR SEED MILKS

Nut milks are often used by people who are either allergic to milk products or want to eliminate the mucous-forming milk products from their diet.

⅓ cup shelled nuts (almonds, cashews, walnuts, brazil, etc.) or seeds (sesame or any variety)
1 cup water

2 tsp. honey or sugar or fruit concentrates, optional
several drops flavor extract, optional

If your juicer has a blank attachment (in place of the screen), you can make nut or seed milks. Otherwise you will have to use a blender or food processor. With the juicer, push nuts slowly through the feed tube, mixing with water as you go. You may need to use a blender afterwards for a smoother consistency. Add sweeteners or flavorings if desired.

If you need to use the blender or food processor, simply grind nuts finely and add water, continuing to process until smooth.

PINA COLADA PUNCH

For the people who love tropical flavors!

1 qt. fresh pineapple juice
1 qt. fresh orange juice
1 qt. 7-Up
½ to 1 can coconut cream
rum to taste, optional

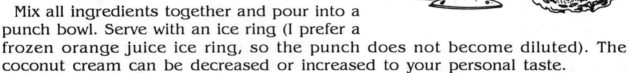

Mix all ingredients together and pour into a punch bowl. Serve with an ice ring (I prefer a frozen orange juice ice ring, so the punch does not become diluted). The coconut cream can be decreased or increased to your personal taste.

NOTE: I tried making my own coconut cream from fresh coconut and found that it was too much work and required an incredible amount of coconut to make a small amount of cream.

HOT FRESH APPLE CIDER PUNCH

Servings: 12

A wonderful fall punch that can be varied according to the type of apples used, the type of alcohol used and the garnish.

1 gal. fresh apple juice
1 oz. cinnamon sticks (broken)
1 oz. cloves, whole
vodka, apple jack, or any apple liqueur to taste
whipped cream or a sprinkle of allspice for garnish

Simmer ingredients over low heat for 20 minutes until flavors combine and juice is hot. Strain and keep hot in crock pot or electric coffee pot. To serve: pour liquor if desired in a cup, add spiced juice and top with whipped cream or sprinkle with spice.

NOTE: You can use vanilla ice cream instead of whipping cream for a different touch!

CHRISTMAS PUNCH

Since Christmas is such a time of sweets, it's nice to serve something actually healthy. Cranberries are a natural diuretic and urinary tract cleanser. So enjoy something tasty and healthy!

1 qt. fresh apple juice
1 qt. fresh cranberry juice
½ cup honey
2 tbs. fresh lemon juice
2 cups plain nonfat yogurt, optional

Place all the ingredients in a blender and process until smooth; chill and serve. The yogurt gives it a creamy quality and if desired, or you can float vanilla ice cream on top for a richer treat.

NOTE: I freeze part of the juice mixture and make it into an ice ring to float in the punch so it won't become diluted during the party.

SPICED GRAPE PUNCH

Servings: 8

Fresh grape juice always surprises people when I first introduce them to it. Try mixing different varieties for a totally new experience! Grape juice stimulates the metabolism, helps cleanse and build the blood, and stimulates the liver.

¾ cup sugar
1¼ cups water
¼ tsp. nutmeg
1 tbs. fresh grated orange peel
1 tbs. fresh grated lemon peel
½ inch slice ginger root, cut in thin slices
1 piece cinnamon stick, 6 inches
6 whole cloves
4 cups fresh grape juice
½ cup fresh orange juice
¼ cup fresh lemon juice

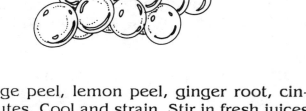

Combine sugar, water, nutmeg, orange peel, lemon peel, ginger root, cinnamon stick and cloves; simmer 10 minutes. Cool and strain. Stir in fresh juices and chill.

BANANA PUNCH

Banana is a very popular flavor in punches, and depending on this flavor of the sherbet used, you can give this a real tropical flavor.

3 cups mashed bananas
1 cup fresh lemon juice
2 cups sugar
2 cups cream, ice cream or plain yogurt
6 cups 7-Up or ginger ale
1 pt. lemon or pineapple sherbet or sorbet
1/3 cup coconut cream, optional

Puree bananas, lemon juice and sugar together in a blender or food processor. Add cream (or ice cream or yogurt) and process until smooth. Pour into a punch bowl and add 7-Up or ginger ale. Scoop flavored sherbets on top. Stir in coconut cream if desired.

DRINKS AND PUNCHES **45**

GUAVA PUNCH

Guava is a real tropical treat and goes well with citrus juices.

3 cups guava nectar
½ cup fresh orange juice
3 tbs. fresh lemon juice
3 cups fresh pineapple juice
1 cup sugar
1 cup water
2 qt. ginger ale
pineapple and orange chunks for garnish

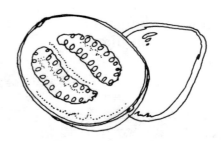

Mix fruit juices together and chill. Heat sugar and water together for several minutes to make a syrup and chill. Add chilled juices and chilled syrup together; pour in ginger ale.

HOT SOUPS AND COLD SOUPS

FRESH TOMATO SOUP

Servings: 6

Once you've tasted fresh tomato soup you'll never go back to canned!

1/4 cup butter
1 small onion, minced
1 clove garlic, minced
1/2 cup carrot pulp
1 can (6 oz.) tomato paste
2 cups fresh tomato juice
1/2 tsp. basil
1/2 tsp. thyme

1/2 tsp. parsley
1/2 cup celery pulp
2 cans (10 oz. each) chicken broth
salt and pepper to taste
2/3 cup heavy cream, optional
 (or garnish each dish with a dollop
 of sour cream)

In a soup kettle, melt butter. Sauté onion, garlic, carrot and celery in butter until limp. Add tomato paste to pan and stir. Add tomato juice and cook for 3 minutes. Add chicken broth and seasonings; simmer for 5 minutes. Correct seasonings to your personal taste. Just before serving, stir in cream or top each dish with a dollop of sour cream if desired.

EASY VEGETABLE BEEF SOUP

Servings: 8

Soups are a great way to use leftover vegetable pulp. Any of the vegetables in this recipe can be interchanged with whatever vegetables you happen to be juicing.

2½ lb. beef shanks
6 cups water
1 cup onion pulp
1 cup celery pulp
1 cup carrot pulp
1 cup potatoes, cubed or potato pulp

1 tbs. salt
¼ tsp. pepper
1 can (16 oz.) green beans, undrained
1 can (16 oz.) corn, undrained
½ cup pasta, uncooked (I like orzo)

In a large soup pan, combine cut-up beef shanks, water, onion pulp, celery pulp, carrot pulp, potatoes, salt and pepper. Bring to a boil, reduce heat, cover and simmer for about 1½ hours. Remove from heat and remove bones, cutting meat into bite-size pieces. Add green beans, corn and pasta. Cover and simmer about 20 minutes. Taste and adjust seasonings to your personal taste.

GAZPACHO

Chilled soups are a delightful change for a starter course and cucumbers are very refreshing. Besides being a natural diuretic, cucumbers are great for the hair and nails.

3 oz. bread crumbs
2 tbs. red wine vinegar
2 cloves garlic, crushed
1 tsp. salt
2 cucumbers, juiced
1 onion, juiced

1 green bell pepper, juiced
¼ cup olive oil
6 tomatoes, juiced
2 cups stock or water
2 to 4 tbs. fresh lemon juice
pepper to taste

Soak bread crumbs in red wine vinegar. Place this mixture in a food processor and blend with garlic, salt, cucumber juice, onion juice and green pepper juice. Add olive oil slowly down the feed tube. Add tomatoes, stock, a little lemon juice and pepper. Taste; adjust seasoning to personal taste. Serve with croutons.

NOTE: The amount of vinegar or lemon juice will change depending on the acidity of the tomatoes, and the amount of stock (or water) necessary will change depending on the juiciness of the tomatoes.

EGG LEMON SOUP

First served to me in a Greek restaurant — and I was hooked. This is a great light starter course.

10 cups chicken stock
1 cup white rice, raw
4 eggs
¼ cup fresh lemon juice
1 tbs. parsley, chopped
salt to taste
chopped parsley for garnish

Bring chicken stock and rice to a boil; cover and simmer 20 minutes, until rice is tender. Beat eggs until frothy and very slowly beat in lemon juice (this will curdle if you add it too quickly). Take about 2 cups of the heated rice mixture and beat it into beaten eggs. Add egg mixture to pan, using a wire whisk. Remove from heat, taste for seasoning and serve immediately sprinkled with a little chopped parsley.

CREAMY CARROT SOUP

Servings: 6

Carrot soup can be served either hot or chilled. It's a great way to use leftover carrots and an unusual surprise to your guests.

3 cups chicken broth
2 cups carrot pulp
½ cup onion pulp or chopped onions
2 tsp. curry powder
¼ tsp. thyme
1 tsp. nutmeg
1 clove garlic, minced
1 cup sour cream
½ cup milk

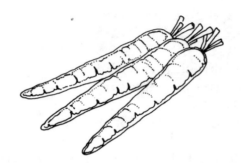

In a saucepan, combine broth, carrot pulp, onion pulp, curry, thyme, nutmeg and garlic. Cover and cook over medium heat for about 10 minutes. Place all ingredients in a blender or food processor and puree until smooth. Return to saucepan and stir in sour cream and milk. Gently heat over low (do not boil) and serve.

MINTY CUCUMBER SOUP

Cucumber soup goes well with a hot summer day. In addition to being tasty, this is great for people with water retention problems during hot weather, because cucumbers are natural diuretics.

3 tbs. butter
½ cup onion pulp
1 clove garlic, minced
1½ cups cucumber pulp
3 tbs. flour

3½ cups chicken stock
2 tbs. fresh mint, finely chopped
½ cup cream
½ cup milk
salt and white pepper to taste

Melt butter in a saucepan. Add onion pulp, garlic and cucumber pulp. Sauté until limp and stir in flour. Add chicken stock, stir and bring to a boil. Reduce heat and simmer for 5 minutes. Place mixture in a blender or food processor and puree until smooth. Stir in fresh mint and chill. Just before serving, stir in cream, milk, salt and white pepper.

HOT SOUPS AND COLD SOUPS **53**

CREAMY BROCCOLI SOUP

Servings: 8

Think of eating this soup on a cold winter day, with a crusty French bread, while you sit in front of a fire.

5 cups broccoli pulp
6 cups chicken stock
5 tbs. butter
⅓ cup flour
1½ cups cream
1½ cups milk
½ tsp. nutmeg
salt and pepper to taste

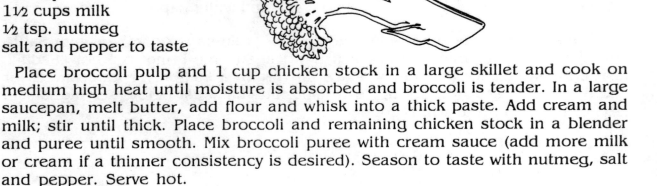

Place broccoli pulp and 1 cup chicken stock in a large skillet and cook on medium high heat until moisture is absorbed and broccoli is tender. In a large saucepan, melt butter, add flour and whisk into a thick paste. Add cream and milk; stir until thick. Place broccoli and remaining chicken stock in a blender and puree until smooth. Mix broccoli puree with cream sauce (add more milk or cream if a thinner consistency is desired). Season to taste with nutmeg, salt and pepper. Serve hot.

CREAMY SPINACH SOUP

Servings: 4

A great way to use leftover spinach and get your vitamins too.

1 cup spinach pulp
1/4 cup water
4 tbs. butter
3 tbs. onion pulp
3 tbs. flour
2 1/2 cups scalded milk

salt and pepper
1/8 tsp. nutmeg
dash Tabasco sauce
2 egg yolks
3/4 cup cream

   Put spinach pulp and water in a saucepan and cook for 5 minutes. Pour into a blender or food processor and blend until smooth. Melt butter in a saucepan and sauté onion pulp until wilted. Sprinkle flour over onions and blend well. Cook for 2 minutes; add scalded milk, stirring until thickened. Puree this mixture in blender or food processor. Stir in pureed spinach. Season with salt, pepper, nutmeg and Tabasco. Taste and adjust to your personal preference. Simmer soup over low heat for several minutes. In a separate bowl, mix egg yolks with cream and slowly add to warm soup, stirring constantly. Serve at once.

CHEESE SOUP

Servings: 6

Cheese soup is always a favorite and this particular recipe uses several different kinds of vegetable pulp. Consider using other combinations of vegetables for variety.

6 tbs. butter
3/4 cup onion pulp
1/2 cup celery pulp
3/4 cup carrot pulp
4 tbs. flour
salt and white pepper to taste
1/2 tsp. paprika

pinch of cayenne
5 cups chicken broth
1 cup cream
2 tbs. sherry
3 cups cheddar cheese, grated
chopped parsley for garnish

Melt butter in a saucepan and sauté onion pulp, celery pulp and carrot pulp for 5 minutes. Sprinkle on flour, salt, white pepper, paprika and cayenne; stir well. Add chicken broth and stir until mixture has thickened. Reduce heat to low, add cream, sherry and cheese, and stir until smooth. Sample and adjust seasoning to your personal taste. Serve hot and garnish with chopped parsley.

CHILLED AROMATIC SOUP

Servings: 6-8

This is a very exotic, unusual chilled soup that is a great starter course for people who appreciate the extraordinary.

½ cup onion pulp
¼ cup carrot pulp
¼ cup celery pulp
5 tbs. butter
1½ tsp. curry powder
1 large cinnamon stick (broken into pieces)
2 bay leaves
1 tsp. whole cloves

5½ cups chicken stock
1 tbs. tomato paste
3 tbs. almond paste
1 tbs. currant jelly
1½ tbs. flour
salt and white pepper to taste
2 cups cream
toasted coconut or toasted almonds for garnish

In a heavy saucepan, sauté onion pulp, carrot pulp and celery pulp in 2 tbs. butter. Add curry, cinnamon stick, bay leaves, whole cloves, chicken broth, tomato paste, almond paste and currant jelly; stir well. Bring to a boil, reduce heat and simmer 1 hour covered. In a separate pan, melt remaining 3 tbs. butter and stir in flour. Gradually add this to soup mixture. Simmer until mixture thickens. Strain and taste for seasonings, adjust to your personal taste and chill. Stir in cream just before serving and garnish.

FRESH PLUM SOUP

Servings: 6

Plum soup can be used as a starter course, palate refresher or a dessert. Guests are always pleasantly surprised at this unique dish.

4½ cups fresh plum juice mixed
   with the plum pulp
¾ cup rusk crumbs
1½ cups dry white wine
1½ cups fresh apple juice
¼ tsp. cinnamon
¼ tsp. cloves

⅛ tsp. ginger
½ to 1 cup sugar
1½ tsp. fresh lemon juice
6 tbs. cream
¾ cup rhine wine
cream or ice cream for garnish

Cook plum juice (with plum pulp), rusk crumbs, white wine, apple juice and spices until plums are soft. Add sugar (adjusting to personal taste depending on tartness of plums) and cook for 5 minutes longer. Place in a blender or food processor and blend until smooth. Add lemon juice, cream and rhine wine. Serve either hot or cold and garnish with a dollop of cream or ice cream.

BLACK CHERRY SOUP

Servings: 4

Besides the great taste of cherry you get the benefits of numerous vitamins and minerals. Cherry reduces the acidity of the blood which is good for gout and arthritis.

2 cups sweet black cherries
3 oranges or apples
2 to 3 tbs. honey
2 cups water
plain yogurt or whipped cream for garnish

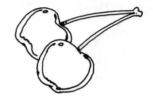

Pit cherries and juice. Remove orange peel (leaving white pith) and juice (or juice apples). Add honey and water and taste, adjusting the sweetness to your personal taste. Served chilled with a dollop of plain yogurt or whipped cream on top.

NOTE: Another possibility is to add the plain yogurt to the soup and blend well.

FRESH BERRY SOUP

Servings: 6

Fruit soups are generally served chilled and garnished with cream or sour cream. I think fruit soup is wonderful starter course for a summer meal.

2 cups fresh berry juice
4 cups water
2 tbs. tapioca
1 tbs. fresh lemon juice
3 tbs. sugar or to taste
¼ cup white wine
whipped cream, cream, sour cream, yogurt or even ice cream and a few fresh
  berries for garnish

Mix berry juice, water and tapioca together and pour into a saucepan. Cook over medium heat until mixture takes on a transparent look. Add lemon juice and sugar. Allow to cool before stirring in wine. Serve chilled with a garnish.

SAUCES, BUTTERS AND MARINADES

SWEET AND SOUR SAUCE

2 quarts

Sweet and sour is such a popular flavor that I make this sauce in large quantities and keep it on hand in the refrigerator.

2¼ cups fresh pineapple juice
4½ tbs. cornstarch
1½ cups cider vinegar
4 tbs. catsup

1½ cups brown sugar
3 cups pineapple pulp
1 tbs. salt
red food coloring, optional

Mix pineapple juice and cornstarch together and bring to a boil. Add remaining ingredients and stir until thickened.

NOTE: I usually keep the skin on the pineapple when juicing in order to get the maximum food value, but when using the pulp in cooking I remove the skin before juicing.

APPLE MUSTARD SAUCE

1½ cups

This is great on chicken or turkey, and fast!

1 onion
2 tbs. butter
1 cup fresh apple juice
1 tsp. fresh lemon juice
1 clove garlic, minced
½ tsp. thyme
1 tsp. sugar
1½ tbs. Dijon mustard

Either slice or dice onion (depending on the texture you would like) and sauté in butter for 3 minutes. Add apple juice, lemon juice, garlic, thyme, and sugar; cook for 10 minutes. Add mustard, taste and adjust to your personal taste.

RASPBERRY SAUCE

1 cup

Raspberry sauce can be used on poached fruit, over ice cream or frozen yogurts, and goes well with rich chocolate desserts.

12 oz. raspberries
¼ cup orange liqueur or juice
2 tsp. fresh lemon juice
sugar or honey to taste

Juice raspberries. Add remaining ingredients, adjusting sweetness to your personal taste. If you use fresh berries it will probably require a lot less sugar than frozen berries. Blend until smooth.

LEMON SAUCE

There are so many things that lemon sauce can be used for; bread pudding, cheesecake, cakes, gingerbread, poached fruit, crepes, soufflés, etc.

½ cup sugar
1½ tbs. cornstarch
1 tbs. grated lemon zest
¼ cup fresh lemon juice
1 cup water

Combine sugar, cornstarch and lemon zest in a saucepan. Whisk in lemon juice and water; bring to a boil, stirring constantly until thickened.

DEMI-GLACE SAUCE

2½ cups

Demi-glace is wonderful sauce for beef or even pork dishes. This has been converted to use the vegetable pulp and can be made in bulk and frozen when you are having a "vegetable juice frenzy!"

3 tbs. vegetable oil
⅓ cup carrot pulp
⅓ cup onion pulp
⅓ cup celery pulp
1 tbs. flour
1 tsp. tomato puree

2 cups beef stock
1 tbs. minced mushroom
1 bouquet garni (thyme sprig, parsley stalks and bay leaf tied together in a bundle)
salt and pepper to taste

Heat oil in a shallow saucepan and add carrot pulp, onion pulp and celery pulp. Cook on low heat until vegetables are barely colored. Then stir in flour and continue to stir until vegetables take on a russet color (about 10 minutes). Add tomato puree, 1½ cups of the beef stock, mushrooms and bouquet garni. Bring to a boil, half cover with a lid and simmer for 25 minutes. Add remaining ½ cup of cold beef stock and skim off fat that rises to the surface. Strain through a sieve, season lightly and taste (adjust seasoning to your personal taste).

CRANBERRY ORANGE SAUCE

This is a quick and simple sauce which goes well with turkey, chicken or even a Christmas goose.

1 cup cranberries
½ cup fresh orange juice
2 to 3 tbs. honey
¼ cup vegetable oil
¾ tsp. cinnamon
1 tbs. red vinegar (I prefer balsamic)

Bring cranberries and orange juice to a boil in a saucepan. Cover and let simmer until cranberries are tender. If you have a blank attachment to your juicer, homogenize mixture together, or use a food processor and blend until smooth. Add honey, oil, cinnamon and vinegar; process until smooth. At this point taste and either add more honey for sweetness or vinegar for tartness.

FRESH LEMON BUTTER SAUCE

When I think of lemon butter sauce, all kinds of seafoods come to mind like lobster, cod, halibut, salmon, etc. One of my friends said she used this for a fresh artichoke dipping sauce.

1 cup butter
¼ cup fresh lemon juice
2 tsp. Worcestershire sauce
pinch of pepper
1 tsp. sugar
2 tsp. parsley pulp or chopped parsley

Melt butter in a saucepan, and add lemon juice, Worcestershire sauce, pepper and sugar. Simmer for 1 to 2 minutes. Remove from heat and add parsley. Serve immediately.

MALAYAN CURRY SAUCE

4 cups

This sauce is great served with broiled tender strips of beef and served over rice. Curry is a touchy spice so always use it moderately to start and increase amount to your personal taste.

1 tbs. curry powder
1 tbs. butter
½ cup onion pulp
½ cup celery pulp
½ cup apple pulp
¾ cup beef stock

1 cup cream
1 cup milk
1 tbs. cornstarch
2 tbs. cold water
salt to taste

Sauté curry powder in butter until brown. Stir in onion pulp, celery pulp and apples; cook for 1 minute. Add beef stock and bring to a boil. Remove from stove and puree in a blender or food processor until smooth. Return to heat and stir in cream and milk — be careful not to boil. Combine cornstarch and cold water; stir into hot mixture. Cook and stir until thick.

MINT SAUCE

I love the flavor of mint, especially with something like a roast pork dinner. This is an excellent sauce for vegetables like carrots, peas, or even sweet potatoes.

4 tbs. butter
½ cup water
2 tsp. cornstarch
1 tbs. sugar
pinch of salt
1 tbs. fresh lemon juice
1 tbs. mint, finely chopped

In a saucepan, melt butter. Combine cornstarch with water, add to melted butter with sugar, salt, lemon juice and mint. Stir until thickened. Taste and adjust flavor to personal tartness or sweetness.

70 SAUCES, BUTTERS AND MARINADES

ORANGE CREAM

2½ cups

Orange cream is a simple way to make a dessert sauce to serve over fresh fruit in the summertime.

½ cup sugar
½ cup fresh orange juice
1 tbs. orange peel, grated, optional
1 cup cream

Bring sugar, orange juice and orange peel to a boil in a saucepan. Stir until sugar is dissolved. Then simmer 10 minutes without stirring (this will make an orange syrup). Remove from heat and chill. Whip cream and gently fold into the orange syrup. Serve over fresh fruit.

BLACKBERRY WHITE WINE SAUCE

1 quart

This delicious sauce was served with trout breaded in hazelnuts. Consider using it with poultry or pork entrées.

3 oz. red wine vinegar
1/4 tsp. white pepper
3 oz. white wine
2 cups butter, chilled
1/2 cup shallots, minced
1 cup blackberry juice (sweetened if desired)

Combine vinegar, white wine, shallots and white pepper in a saucepan and reduce to approximately 1/2 cup. Slowly whisk in chilled butter, stirring constantly. Add blackberry juice. Taste and adjust flavor to your own personal taste.

APPLE BUTTER

1 quart

When apple season is at its peak, this is a great way to use the apples and produce a healthy alternative to sugary jams.

2 lb. tart apples
1½ cups brown sugar or to taste
1 cup fresh apple juice
½ tsp. cinnamon
½ lemon (including peel)

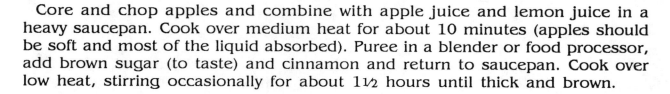

Core and chop apples and combine with apple juice and lemon juice in a heavy saucepan. Cook over medium heat for about 10 minutes (apples should be soft and most of the liquid absorbed). Puree in a blender or food processor, add brown sugar (to taste) and cinnamon and return to saucepan. Cook over low heat, stirring occasionally for about 1½ hours until thick and brown.

NUT BUTTERS

Nut butters have gained popularity recently and now you have the capability of making your own. Certain juicers have a blank plate that attaches to the machine in place of the screen which allows the mixture to be processed through the grating disk, but a food processor can also be used.

nuts; peanuts, roasted cashews, raw or roasted walnuts, (optional toasting can add a totally different flavor) almonds, raw or roasted, hazelnuts, raw or roasted, macadamia nuts, raw or roasted
oil (variety depending on the oil content of the nut)
salt, optional
sweetener; honey, sugar or molasses, optional

With the blank screen in place, simply drop the *shelled* nuts down the feed tube of the juicer. If the mixture is too dry, dribble a little oil of your choice down the tube with the nuts while grinding. Depending on the speed at which you push the nuts down the tube, you will be able to get either creamy (with slow action) or crunchy (with a faster action). You may use salted nuts or add a little salt to the nuts while grinding so that the salt mixes in evenly (this is totally optional to your personal taste). Sweetener is also an option for those used to the sweeter peanut butters sold in grocery stores.

If your juicer doesn't have a removable screen, then use a food processor. Using the double steel blade, simply process the nuts for several minutes. Again, if the mixture is too dry, add a little oil. Then add the optional salt and/or sweetener and process for 30 seconds longer.

LEMON PEPPER BUTTER

1 cup

Flavored butters are a great change and impress your guests. Consider using this on baked potatoes or on herb breads.

1 cup butter
2 tbs. minced chives
1 tsp. grated lemon peel
2 tbs. fresh lemon juice
1/4 tsp. pepper

Cream butter until soft. Add remaining ingredients and mix well. Chill.

LEMON BUTTER JELLY

3 cups

A quick and easy spread to use over toast, muffins, or even as a filling for tarts or pastries.

4 eggs, beaten
½ cup fresh lemon juice
2½ cups sugar
1 tbs. butter

Mix eggs, lemon juice and sugar together and place in a double boiler. Cook until mixture thickens, stirring occasionally. Remove from heat and stir in butter. Cool and refrigerate.

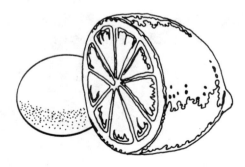

ROSE MARINADE

1½ cups

This is a great marinade for lamb that has an unusual ingredient of rose petals (which are high in vitamin C).

10 red roses (without the stems)
1 cup fresh orange juice
4 tbs. sugar

4 tbs. mint jelly
4 tbs. cognac or orange liqueur

Separate petals of roses and wash well. In a saucepan, combine rose petals, orange juice, sugar, and mint jelly. Simmer on low for 45 minutes. Add cognac or liqueur (adjusting to your personal taste) and stir for 2 minutes. Cool and strain. Brush over lamb at least 1 hour before roasting.

NOTE: If roses are unavailable or too expensive, rose water can be substituted. Rose water can usually be found in gourmet cooking shops or sometimes in specialty spice shops.

ORANGE SOY MARINADE

1½ cups

This is a great marinade for poultry dishes (chicken, cornish hens, duck, and goose) especially if you are planning to broil or barbecue.

¾ cup fresh orange juice
½ cup soy sauce
2½ tbs. honey
2 tbs. onion, minced
1 tbs. grated orange rind
1 tsp. dry mustard
1 tsp. curry powder
1 tbs. parsley, finely chopped
½ tsp. cayenne

Mix all ingredients together in a blender or food processor and blend well. Place marinade on poultry and refrigerate. This marinade is also good to use for basting.

BEEF TOMATO MARINADE

2¾ cups

A great marinade for beef that uses fresh tomato juice.

2 cups fresh tomato juice
⅔ cup vinegar (I like balsamic vinegar)
2 tbs. oil
2 tbs. horseradish
2 tsp. sugar
1 tsp. salt
¼ tsp. pepper

   Mix all ingredients together in a blender or food processor. Taste and adjust seasonings. This makes enough marinade to cover about 4 pounds of meat. Marinate for 6 to 8 hours before broiling or barbecuing.

TANGY PORK GLAZE

4 cups

The citrus juices are a great compliment to pork products. This recipe is sweet with a slight tang.

1⅓ cups ketchup
1 cup orange marmalade
¾ cup onion pulp
½ cup fresh lemon juice
½ cup soy sauce
1 tsp. marjoram
½ tsp. pepper
salt to taste (add if not using salt on the meat directly)

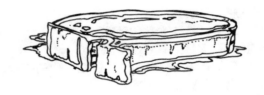

Combine all ingredients in a saucepan and heat, stirring well. Apply this glaze to roast in the last 40 minutes of cooking, basting every 10 minutes. This glaze can also be served as a side sauce.

DRESSINGS

COCONUT DRESSING

Use this recipe as a fruit salad dressing or a dip. By changing the flavor of the yogurt and using different kinds of citrus fruits, you can create endless variations of this recipe.

½ cup coconut cream
1 tsp. ginger root juice
1 tbs. fresh lime juice or lemon juice

1 tbs. honey
½ cup yogurt, (plain, lime- or lemon-
  flavored)

Use either canned or homogenized coconut cream. To homogenize coconut, remove shell, peel thin brown shell with a potato peeler and cut into strips that fit the juicing tube. Insert the blank screen attachment and push through the grating disk (adding water if coconut meat seems a little dry).

If you do not have this attachment, use canned coconut cream. Stir in remaining ingredients and adjust to your personal sweetness.

FRUIT SALAD DRESSING

2 cups

This makes a wonderful thick fruit custard that is a nice alternative to whipped cream for fruit salads. It may be stored in the refrigerator for several days.

½ cup fresh orange juice
1 cup fresh pineapple juice
½ cup sugar
¼ cup cornstarch
⅓ cup water
1 tbs. butter

Bring orange juice, pineapple juice and sugar to a boil. Mix cornstarch with water and add to hot juice mixture. Boil until thickened, stirring constantly. Remove from heat and stir in butter. Cool and stir into prepared fruit salad mix.

ORANGE VINAIGRETTE

3 cups

This is a nice alternative to your regular oil and vinegar dressing. It's good on tossed salads containing fruit as a sweet and sour dressing for spinach salads.

¾ cup fresh orange juice
¾ cup vinegar
1½ cups olive oil (or blend of oils)
2 tbs. grated orange zest
1 tbs. soy sauce
1 tbs. sugar, optional

Pour all ingredients into a food processor or blender and mix. Sugar (or honey) may be added if you like a more sweet and sour flavor.

LOW CALORIE TOMATO DRESSING

3/4 cups

This is a great recipe for calorie watchers, as well as the health conscious. Add a little oregano for a more Italian flavor.

6 oz. fresh tomato juice
2 cloves garlic, minced
1 tbs. soy sauce
dash of Tabasco sauce
1 tsp. salt
1 tsp. basil
1½ tsp. pepper

Pour all ingredients into a food processor or blender and mix until well blended.

CREAMY CHUTNEY DRESSING

Chutney creates a unique flavor that I believe enhances fruit salad or tossed salads with fruit ingredients.

½ cup plain yogurt or sour cream
2 tbs. fresh apple juice
2 tbs. chutney
1 tsp. fresh lemon juice, optional

Mix all ingredients together in a food processor or blender. Taste adjust sweetness to your personal taste.

LEMON MINT DRESSING

2¼ cups

I'm always looking for a different dressing for fruit salad. Mint is a refreshing change and is a good aid to digestion.

¼ cup mint, finely chopped
1 tbs. sugar
2 cups sour cream
1 tbs. fresh lemon juice
¼ tsp. salt

Mix mint and sugar together and let sit for 10 minutes. Fold in sour cream, lemon juice and salt. Taste and adjust to personal sweetness. Chill.

FRENCH DRESSING

2¼ cups

Another version of French dressing using fresh lemon juice. I prefer to use balsamic vinegar for a more refined taste.

1 cup sugar
¼ cup vinegar
½ cup vegetable oil
2 to 3 cloves garlic, crushed
3 tbs. fresh lemon juice
½ cup catsup
salt to taste

   Put all ingredients into a blender and mix well. Taste and adjust the sweetness or tartness to your personal taste.

MANGO VINAIGRETTE

1½ cups

Here's a totally different dressing that goes great on tossed salads with exotic tropical fruits like mangos or papayas.

3 mangos
6 tbs. sesame oil
6 tbs. rice vinegar
1 tsp. curry powder

Remove seeds from mangos and juice (leaving peeling on). Mix mango juice with sesame oil, vinegar and curry in a blender or food processor. Refrigerate until ready to serve.

NOTE: I have found that the best way to deseed a mango is to cut the two sides off leaving the seed with a rim of mango meat around it. Then I cut the seed out of the middle and juice the rest.

PESTO SALAD DRESSING

Pesto is very popular flavor and can be used on pasta salads, pasta entrée dishes, fish dishes, and salad dressings.

1 egg
½ cup olive oil

2 tbs. lemon juice
½ cup pesto sauce

To make the salad dressing, simply place egg, olive oil, lemon juice and pesto sauce in a food processor or blender and mix. This is one of my favorite dressings for pasta salad. Taste and adjust for tartness. If the lemon is overpowering, simply add a little sugar to compensate.

PESTO SAUCE

2 cups fresh basil leaves
6 parsley sprigs
3 tbs. pine nuts

2 cloves garlic, minced
½ cup Parmesan cheese
½ cup olive oil

To make the pesto sauce, place basil leaves in a food processor with parsley and spin until finely chopped. Add remaining ingredients and mix until well blended.

COLD AND FROSTY DESSERTS

LEMON ICE

This is a wonderful way to cleanse the palate after a rather heavy meal or just to have as a light dessert served with a crisp cookie.

zest from 2 lemons
1 cup sugar
dash of salt
2/3 cup lemon juice
4 cups water

Remove zest from lemons with a potato peeler (or zester) and place in a processor with sugar. Process until finely ground. Combine with salt, lemon juice and water in a small saucepan. Heat to boiling and stir to dissolve sugar. Freeze in an ice cube tray. To serve, process several cubes at a time until light and fluffy. Place in scooped-out lemon halves and garnish with mint.

COLD AND FROSTY DESSERTS **93**

PAPAYA ICE

Papayas are known for their wonderful digestive properties. This can be used after a heavy meat meal to help digest the protein.

1½ cups papaya, cubed
1 tbs. fresh lemon juice
1½ cups fresh orange juice
1 cup sugar
2 cups milk, plain yogurt or cream

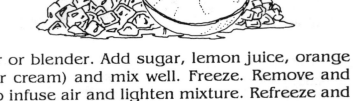

Puree papaya in a food processor or blender. Add sugar, lemon juice, orange juice, sugar and milk (or yogurt or cream) and mix well. Freeze. Remove and cut into cubes and process again to infuse air and lighten mixture. Refreeze and serve.

SUPER LEMON MOUSSE

Servings: 12

This is a luscious creamy mousse with an intense lemon flavor, perfect as a light dessert after a heavy meal.

1 pkg. unflavored gelatin
4 tbs. cold water
3 tbs. cornstarch
1¼ cups sugar
1 cup fresh lemon juice

½ cup fresh orange juice
5 egg yolks, beaten
8 egg whites
2 cups cream, whipped
2 tbs. grated lemon zest

In a heavy stainless steel (not aluminum) saucepan, soften gelatin in 2 tbs. cold water. In a separate dish, dissolve cornstarch in remaining 2 tbs. cold water. Add sugar, lemon juice and orange juice to gelatin and heat gently. Add dissolved cornstarch and stir to thicken. Pour a little of this heated mixture into beaten egg yolks, return the whole mixture to saucepan and stir until thick. Remove from heat and let cool completely.

Beat egg whites until stiff peaks form (but not dry). Gently fold gelatin into egg whites until completely incorporated. Then fold in whipped cream and finally lemon zest. Pour into serving dishes and refrigerate 3 to 4 hours or until set.

RASPBERRY SHERBET

Servings: 6

Raspberry is such a popular flavor and sherbet is such a nice light dessert that this makes the perfect summer finish to a meal. But also consider it in winter, using frozen berries.

¾ cup water
1 cup sugar
4 cups fresh raspberries
3 tbs. powdered sugar

1 tbs. raspberry liqueur, optional
1 pkg. unflavored gelatin
¼ cup water
½ egg white

Heat ¾ cup water and sugar together over low heat until dissolved; bring to a boil for 4 minutes. Let syrup cool. Juice raspberries and beat in powdered sugar. Gradually stir in cool sugar syrup into puree and add raspberry liqueur, if desired. Taste and adjust to personal sweetness. Sprinkle gelatin over ¼ cup water and let stand for 5 minutes. Dissolve it over low heat and stir into raspberry mixture. Chill mixture in an ice cube tray until slushy. Stiffly beat egg white and add to chilled fruit mixture. Cover tightly and chill again, beating once or twice more to break up ice crystals as sherbet freezes.

COLD LEMON SOUFFLÉ
WITH RASPBERRY SAUCE

I love the tang of lemon with the sweetness of raspberries and often finish off a meal with a fruity light dessert.

1 pkg. unflavored gelatin
1/4 cup cold water
5 eggs, separated
3/4 cup fresh lemon juice
1 tbs. grated lemon zest

1 1/2 cups sugar
1 cup cream, whipped
2 pkg. frozen raspberries
sugar to taste
2 tbs. raspberry liqueur

Sprinkle gelatin over cold water and let soften for 5 minutes. Mix egg yolks with lemon juice, zest and 3/4 cup sugar. Place in a heavy saucepan (not aluminum) and cook, stirring constantly until slightly thickened (about 5 minutes). Remove from heat and stir in gelatin until dissolved; chill. Beat egg whites until stiff and add remaining 3/4 cup sugar. Whip cream and combine with lemon mixture and egg whites. Pour into a 2-quart soufflé dish and chill overnight. Juice raspberries, sweeten to taste and add raspberry liqueur if desired. Serve with (or alongside) lemon soufflé.

LEMON CURD

Lemon curd is a strongly flavored lemon pudding that is commonly used in tarts, pies, pastries, etc.

1 cup sugar
¼ lb. butter
2 large lemons (juice and zest)
3 eggs, beaten

Place sugar, butter, and lemon juice into a nonaluminum double boiler and stir until sugar and butter are melted. Add eggs and continue stirring until mixture thickens. Refrigerate until it sets.

NOTE: If the mixture gets too hot it may curdle; if this happens, process the mixture in a food processor until smooth.

CRANBERRY CHAMPAGNE SORBET

Servings: 10

This sorbet can be a light holiday dessert or it can be served during the meal as a palate refresher.

1 tbs. unflavored gelatin
2 cups fresh cranberry juice
2 cups champagne
1 cup sugar (or to taste)
1 tbs. fresh lemon juice

Place gelatin in a large saucepan and cover with ¼ cup cranberry juice. Let stand 5 minutes to soften. Stir in remaining ingredients (taste for sweetness and adjust to personal taste) and place over medium heat. Stir occasionally, until gelatin and sugar are completely dissolved. Pour into a 9-inch square pan and cool. Cover and freeze for several hours. Spoon into a food processor and process, using the double steel blade, until light. Freeze again. To serve, spoon into small glasses and garnish with mint or holly.

FRESH GRAPEFRUIT SORBET

Servings: 6

Grapefruit sorbet is a wonderful palate refresher, starter course or light dessert, but also consider it as a refreshing beginning for the morning, served with fresh grapefruit sections or with croissants.

3 large grapefruits
2/3 cup sugar
1/2 cup fresh grapefruit juice

Dismember grapefruits and puree in a food processor or blender. Place grapefruit puree, sugar and juice into a saucepan and simmer for 20 minutes. Freeze. Cut up, process again and refreeze. Serve in small scoops.

NOTE: For a dessert sorbet, you can add a few tablespoons of Creme de Menthe for a little "spark."

BANANA ORANGE SORBET

Bananas and oranges are a great combination and loaded with potassium. Sorbets are a great light dessert.

1 cup water
1 cup sugar
3 to 4 bananas, frozen

1½ cups fresh orange juice
3 tbs. fresh lemon juice

Heat water and sugar in a saucepan to a boil. Remove from heat and chill. Puree bananas; add chilled sugar syrup, orange juice and lemon juice. Pour into a shallow container and freeze. Cut into pieces and process to lighten and break up the crystals. Refreeze and serve.

BERRY SORBET

Berry sorbets are colorful, full of vitamins and a great light dessert after a heavy meal or served with brunch.

4 cups fresh berry juice
1 cup sugar
1 cup water
berry liqueur, optional

Combine sugar and water in a saucepan and heat until sugar is dissolved. Remove from heat and chill. Add chilled sugar syrup "to taste" to berry juice (depending on the sweetness of the berry). At this point, if you desire, add berry liqueur. Mix and freeze.

Remove from freezer, cut into chunks and process with a blender or food processor to lighten. Refreeze and serve.

NOTE: If you happen to add too much sugar syrup, simply add some fresh lemon juice to compensate.

HAWAIIAN FROZEN POPS

Servings: 6

Any of the juices can be frozen and turned into natural popsicles, but consider mixing several delicious fruits together with mashed bananas and creating a real tropical treat.

½ cup fresh strawberry juice
½ cup fresh pineapple juice
2 ripe bananas, mashed
1½ cups milk, yogurt or cream

Place all ingredients in a blender or food processor and mix well. Taste and depending on sweetness of fruit, you may want to either increase the juice of your choice or add sweetener to your personal taste if desired. Place in an ice cube tray, paper cups or popsicle holders (if available) and insert a wooden stick for the handle. Freeze and serve.

NATURAL SNOW CONES

Some juicers have the capability of removing the screen so that you can grate produce as an option. If your machine has this, you can make snow cones very easily. If not, try using a food processor as an alternative.

ice cubes
fruit juices (any berry, pineapple, melons, mangos, oranges, lemons, cherries, grapes, peaches, pears, or even apples)
sweetener, optional

Remove screen from juicer. Add ice cubes, one at a time through the feed tube (do not force). When you have enough to make several cones, put into a dish or paper cone and drizzle on your favorite flavor of fruit juice (sweetened if desired).

If your machine doesn't have a removable screen, use a food processor, dropping the ice down the feed tube one at a time with the machine running. You may need to stop, scrape the sides for larger chunks of ice and process again.

CREAMY PEAR FREEZE

Servings: 8

When pears are in season, I can't wait to juice them, poach them or puree them. They are a great dessert that people have a tendency to neglect.

2¼ cups fresh pear juice (I prefer Bartletts)
½ cup fresh pineapple juice
1 cup sugar
½ tsp. salt
3 to 4 oz. cream cheese
½ cup cream
2 tbs. fresh lemon juice

Juice pears (leaving peeling and stem on). Alternate with pineapple wedges so machine won't get clogged. In a food processor or blender, mix pear juice, pineapple juice, sugar, salt, cream cheese, cream and lemon juice together and process until smooth. Freeze in a shallow tray. Cut into chunks and run through processor again. Refreeze and serve.

YOGURT POPSICLES

Servings: 6

Frozen yogurt has become an incredibly popular dessert. Yogurt is better for digestion than ice cream and when mixed with natural fruit juices, you've got a great treat for the kids or yourself!

2 cups yogurt, plain or any flavor
1 cup fruit juice, any flavor
1 to 2 tbs. sweetener (honey, sugar, or other), optional

Simply mix all ingredients together and taste. Adjust to personal sweetness. Pour into ice cube trays, paper cups or molds, insert a stick for a handle and freeze until hard.

FROM THE BAKERY

CARROT CAKE

This is one of my favorite recipes for carrot cake, because it stays so moist and the pineapple gives it an different twist.

2 cups sugar
1 tsp. salt
4 eggs
2 tsp. cinnamon
1½ cups vegetable oil
2 cups carrot pulp
2 cups flour
½ cup carrot juice
2 tsp. baking soda
1 cup crushed pineapple, undrained
2 tsp. baking powder
1½ cups chopped nuts

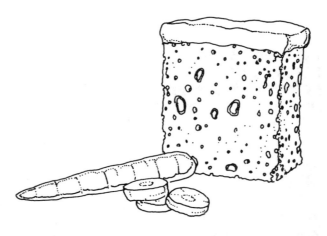

Preheat oven to 350°. Beat together sugar, eggs and oil. Mix flour, soda, baking powder, salt and cinnamon together and add to egg mixture. Add carrot pulp, carrot juice, pineapple and nuts; mix well. Pour into a 9-inch x 13-inch pan and bake for 45 minutes. Cool completely before icing.

CREAM CHEESE ICING

3 oz. cream cheese
½ cup butter
1 box powdered sugar
1 tsp. vanilla extract
pinch of salt
½ cup chopped nuts, optional

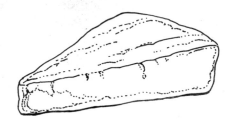

Beat cream cheese and butter together. Beat in powdered sugar, vanilla and salt. Spread on cooled cake and garnish with chopped nuts.

APPLE SPICE CAKE

Servings: 10

A wonderful fall dessert, this tastes even better with an apple glaze made from mixing a little fresh apple juice and fresh lemon juice with powdered sugar and drizzled over the cooled cake.

½ cup butter
1 cup brown sugar
1 egg
2 cups raisins or currants
1 cup walnuts or pecans
1¾ cups flour
½ tsp. salt

1 tsp. baking soda
¾ tsp. cinnamon
½ tsp. cloves
½ tsp. nutmeg
1 cup apple pulp (core removed)
¼ cup fresh apple juice

Preheat oven to 350°. Cream butter and sugar together, add egg and mix well. Coarsely chop nuts and mix with raisins in a separate bowl. Mix flour, salt, baking soda, cinnamon, cloves and nutmeg together, and reserve about ½ cup to mix with raisin and nut mixture. Beat remaining flour mixture with creamed butter. Add apple pulp and apple juice; beat well. Stir in raisin mixture and pour into a buttered bundt pan. Bake 35 to 40 minutes. Remove from oven, cool 10 minutes, remove from pan and cool on a rack.

APPLE DATE CAKE

The dates make this unique and the apples give it that special moistness. I like to frost this with a brown sugar frosting and sprinkle with some chopped nuts.

2 cups sugar
½ cup butter
2 eggs
1 tsp. vanilla
2 cups flour
1 tsp. baking soda

1 tsp. salt
1 tsp. baking powder
1 cup dates, chopped
1 cup chopped nuts
4 cups apple pulp
¾ cup fresh apple juice, water or milk

Preheat oven to 350°. Generously grease a 9-inch x 13-inch pan. Cream sugar and butter together. Add eggs and vanilla; beat well. Mix flour, baking soda, salt and baking powder together and add to creamed mixture. Add dates, nuts, apple pulp and juice; mix. Bake for 45 minutes to 1 hour (depending on moisture in pulp). Cool and frost.

NOTE: If dates are not available, raisins can be substituted.

ZUCCHINI CAKE

Servings: 12

Zucchini cake is such a flavorful way to use plain zucchini. You can substitute other produce like carrots or even apples.

2½ cups flour
1 cup sugar
1 cup brown sugar
1½ tsp. cinnamon
1 tsp. ginger
½ tsp. allspice
½ tsp. nutmeg
1 tsp. salt
1 tsp. baking soda

¼ tsp. baking powder
2 cups zucchini pulp
1 cup vegetable oil
2 tsp. vanilla
3 eggs
¼ cup milk or water
1 cup chopped nuts
½ cup coconut

Preheat oven to 350°. Grease and flour a tube pan. Blend all ingredients together except nuts and coconut. Mix at high speed for 2 minutes. Fold in nuts and coconut. Pour into prepared pan and bake for 50 to 60 minutes. Test for doneness by inserting a knife in the center. When cool, drizzle with glaze.

GLAZE

1½ cups powdered sugar
2 tbs. milk
1 tsp. vanilla

Mix all ingredients together until smooth and drizzle over cooled cake.

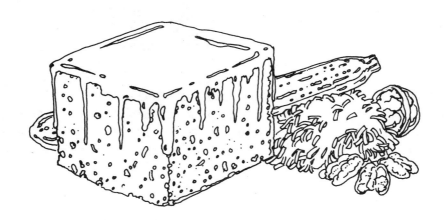

LEMON CREPES

This is one of my very favorite desserts. Even though crepes can be a little time-consuming, they can be made ahead of time, filled and ready for the sauce just before heating. They make an incredible finish to an elegant meal.

CREPE BATTER

4 eggs
1 cup milk
1 cup water
1 tsp. sugar

1/2 tsp. salt
1 tsp. vanilla
4 tbs. butter, melted
2 cups flour

Beat eggs until whites and yolks are well blended. Beat in milk, water, sugar, salt, vanilla and butter. Gradually beat in flour. Let rest for 30 minutes. Just before using, strain through a sieve to remove any lumps and aerate batter. Cook crepes in a lightly buttered skillet over medium high heat and set aside.

FILLING

6 egg yolks
2/3 cup sugar
4 tbs. cornstarch

2 cups milk
1 tsp. fresh lemon juice or vanilla
1 tbs. lemon zest

Combine egg yolks and sugar and whisk mixture until it is pale yellow and forms a ribbon. Stir in cornstarch until it is dissolved. Heat milk and whisk into yolk mixture, constantly stirring until sauce is very thick. Remove from heat; add lemon juice or vanilla and lemon zest. Chill for several hours. Place a tablespoon of filling on each crepe and fold into a wedge-shaped piece. Place crepes, overlapping, in a buttered baking dish.

SAUCE

6 tbs. butter
3/4 cup sugar

2/3 cup fresh lemon juice
1 tbs. lemon zest

Combine butter and sugar in a heavy nonaluminum saucepan. When butter is melted, add lemon juice and zest, whisking until sugar is dissolved. Simmer 3 minutes. Spoon sauce over crepes. Cover with foil and bake in 325° oven for 20 minutes. Just before serving, sprinkle crepes with powdered sugar and place under broiler until sugar is melted and carmelized. Serve immediately.

FRESH ORANGE FLAN

Servings: 8

Fresh orange juice gives this flan a wonderful new twist and the addition of cream cheese gives it the creaminess of cheesecake without all the work.

1 cup sugar (for carmelizing)
8 eggs
2 cans sweetened condensed milk

2 cups fresh orange juice
1 tbs. fresh orange zest
4 oz. cream cheese, softened

Place sugar in a deep pan and place over a medium-high heat, stirring constantly until sugar melts and turns into a light golden syrup. Immediately remove from heat and pour into a warmed round or oval casserole dish. Tilt dish until bottom is entirely coated.

Place remaining ingredients in a blender or food processor and process until very smooth. Pour into prepared dish and cover with aluminum foil. Place dish in a water bath and bake at 350° for 45 minutes, or until a knife inserted into center comes out clean. Chill for several hours. To serve, turn out on a platter.

NOTE: An orange-flavored liqueur can be heated, flamed and served over the flan for a special treat.

PINEAPPLE COOKIES

5 dozen

These remind me of the old-fashioned cookies my grandmother used to make. If you like a little crunch, add about ½ cup of Rice Krispies or any crisp cereal to the batter.

1 cup sugar
1 cup brown sugar
1 cup butter
2 eggs, beaten
1¼ cups pineapple pulp
2 tsp. vanilla

4 cups flour
1 tsp. baking soda
1 tsp. baking powder
½ tsp. salt
1 cup chopped nuts

Preheat oven to 350°. Cream sugars and butter together. Add beaten egg, pineapple pulp and vanilla; mix well. In a separate bowl, combine flour, baking soda, baking powder and salt. Add this to butter mixture and mix well. Stir in chopped nuts. Drop by teaspoonful onto a greased cookie sheet and bake for 12 to 15 minutes.

CARROT COOKIES

4 dozen

Carrots give these cookies a delightful moisture — orange icing adds a tangy spark.

1 cup butter
3/4 cup sugar
2 eggs
1 cup carrot pulp
1/4 cup fresh carrot juice
2 cups flour
2 tsp. baking powder
1 tsp. cinnamon
1/2 tsp. cloves
1/2 tsp. allspice
1/2 tsp. salt
1 cup chopped nuts
1/2 cup raisins

Preheat oven to 400°. Mix butter, sugar, eggs, carrot pulp and carrot juice thoroughly. Add flour, baking powder, cinnamon, cloves, allspice and salt; mix well. Stir in nuts and raisins. Drop dough by spoonfuls onto greased cookie sheets about 2 inches apart. Bake about 8 minutes (test for doneness). Cool and frost with orange icing.

ORANGE ICING

¼ cup butter
3 tbs. fresh orange juice
3 cups powdered sugar
1 tsp. grated fresh orange zest, optional

Beat butter to soften. Add powdered sugar, orange juice and orange zest; beat well.

LEMON BARS

18 bars

These are very easy and have an incredible lemon flavor.

1½ cups butter
⅛ tsp. salt
¾ cup powdered sugar
3 cups flour
6 eggs, beaten
3 cups sugar
⅓ cup flour
⅔ cup fresh lemon juice

Preheat oven to 350°. Mix together butter, salt, powdered sugar and 3 cups flour; press into a 9-inch-x-13-inch pan. Bake for 15 minutes. Combine eggs, 3 cups sugar, ⅓ cup flour and lemon juice together and pour over baked crust. Bake for an additional 25 minutes.

120 FROM THE BAKERY

APPLE CHEESE BREAD

This is one of my all-time favorites. The combination of cheddar cheese and apples makes this very unique tasting and your guests keep wondering why they can't stop eating it.

½ cup butter
⅔ cup sugar
2 eggs, beaten
1¼ cups apple pulp
¼ cup apple juice
¾ cup cheddar cheese, grated

2 cups flour, sifted
1 tsp. baking powder
½ tsp. baking soda
½ tsp. salt
½ cup chopped nuts

Preheat oven to 350°. Prepare a loaf pan by lining with buttered brown paper and buttering sides of pan. Beat butter, sugar and eggs until fluffy. Beat in apple pulp, apple juice and cheddar cheese. Mix flour, baking powder, baking soda and salt together and stir into apple mixture. Then stir in chopped nuts. Pour into prepared loaf pan and bake for 50 to 60 minutes. Cool 10 minutes in pan; remove and cool on a wire rack.

CRANBERRY BREAD

Great for Thanksgiving or Christmas! It's colorful, healthy and tastes good.

2 cups flour
1¼ cups sugar
1½ tsp. baking powder
½ tsp. baking soda
1 tsp. salt
¾ cup fresh orange juice
2 tbs. butter, melted
1 egg, beaten
2 cups cranberry pulp
½ cup chopped nuts

Preheat oven to 350°. Place a piece of buttered brown paper in the bottom of a loaf pan and butter sides of pan. Mix flour, sugar, baking powder, baking soda and salt together. In a separate bowl, combine orange juice, butter and egg. Mix this with flour mixture until just moistened. Fold in cranberry pulp and nuts. At this point, if mixture appears too thick, add a little more fresh orange juice. Spoon into prepared loaf pan. Bake 50 to 60 minutes.

ORANGE BREAD

This is yeast bread with a gentle orange flavor that makes wonderful toast, especially if you serve it with delicious orange butter.

1 tbs. yeast
1/4 cup warm water (115°)
1 tbs. sugar
3 to 4 cups flour
2/3 cup fresh orange juice

1/2 cup orange pulp
2 tbs. sugar
1 tsp. salt
3 tbs. butter, melted

Let yeast soften in warm water for 5 minutes. Add sugar and enough flour (approximately 1/3 cup) to make a thick paste. Beat with a wooden spoon for 1 minute. Cover with plastic wrap and let rise for about 1/2 hour in a warm place. Then add orange juice, orange pulp, 2 tbs. sugar, salt, butter and enough flour to make dough somewhat sticky (but does not stick to the fingers). Knead until smooth and elastic. Shape and let rise again in a greased loaf pan. Bake at 375° for 30 minutes or until bread sounds hollow when thumped.

ORANGE BUTTER
1/2 cup butter

1/4 cup orange marmalade

Let butter soften to room temperature and beat in orange marmalade.

VEGETABLE BREAD

This is a great way to use up your vegetable pulp. By varying the spices and the type of vegetables you use, you can create a totally different flavor each time.

1 tbs. yeast
¾ cup warm water (ll5°)
1 tbs. sugar
4 cups flour
1 cup whole wheat flour
1 egg
1 tsp. salt
1 tbs. basil
½ tsp. thyme, optional
1 tbs. vegetable oil
⅓ cup Parmesan cheese
2 cups vegetable pulp (carrot, celery, onion, green pepper, etc. or a combination)

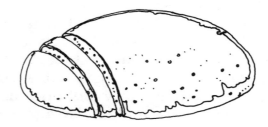

Soften yeast in warm water for 5 minutes. Add sugar and enough flour (approximately 1 to 1½ cups) to make a sponge (the mixture should look like pancake batter). Beat with a wooden spoon for about 1 minute, cover with plastic wrap and let sit for approximately ½ hour in a warm space until sponge has doubled in bulk. Take about ½ cup flour and mix with vegetable pulp (this will help to incorporate vegetables with dough). Mix remaining flours, egg, salt, basil, thyme, oil and cheese together with sponge and beat in vegetable pulp. Knead until dough is smooth and elastic. Shape into a round loaf and place on a greased baking sheet. Let rise until double in bulk. Bake in a 350° oven for 40 to 45 minutes.

NOTE: Depending on the moisture in the air, the amount of flour needed in yeast bread recipes varies. The dough should be sticky but not stick to your fingers. Incorporate only enough flour until you reach this consistency.

ZUCCHINI BREAD

Zucchini bread is another great way to use excessive amounts of zucchini when it is in season. Consider substituting other vegetables or combining several kinds of produce.

2 cups flour
1 cup whole wheat flour
½ tsp. salt
½ tsp. baking powder
1 tsp. baking soda
1 tbs. cinnamon
¼ tsp. nutmeg
3 eggs

1 cup vegetable oil
1½ cups brown sugar
1 tbs. vanilla
2 cups zucchini pulp
¼ cup milk or water
1 cup raisins
1 cup chopped nuts

Preheat oven to 350°. Line 2 loaf pans with buttered brown paper and butter sides of pans. Mix together flours, salt, baking powder, baking soda, cinnamon and nutmeg. In a separate bowl, mix eggs, oil, brown sugar, vanilla, zucchini pulp and milk. Mix flour mixture with zucchini mixture. Stir in raisins and nuts. Pour into prepared pans and bake for 50 to 60 minutes. Cool for 10 minutes on a wire rack; remove from pans.

APPLE MOCHA BREAD

Makes 1 loaf

The combination of chocolate, coffee and apples creates a unique, moist bread that goes well with morning coffee or teas.

½ cup strong coffee, chilled
1 tsp. baking soda
1½ cups flour
½ tsp. salt
½ tsp. cloves
1 tsp. cinnamon

½ cup butter
1 cup sugar
2 eggs
1 oz. unsweetened chocolate
1 cup apple pulp
½ cup raisins

Preheat oven to 350°. Prepare a loaf pan by lining with buttered brown paper and buttering sides of pan. Mix coffee and baking soda together. Combine flour, salt, cloves, and cinnamon; set aside. Beat butter and sugar together until fluffy and mix in eggs, one at a time. Melt chocolate and stir into butter mixture. Then add flour mixture alternately with coffee mixture to butter mixture. Stir in apple pulp and raisins; pour into prepared loaf pan. Bake for 50 to 60 minutes. Cool for 10 minutes; remove from pan and cool on a rack.

CARROT BREAD

Makes 2 loaves

A wonderful way to use leftover carrot pulp. This bread stays moist and freezes very well.

1 cup butter
½ cup sugar
½ cup brown sugar
3 eggs
2 cups flour
1 tsp. baking powder
1 tsp. baking soda

1 tsp. salt
1½ tsp. cinnamon
½ tsp. nutmeg
3 cups carrot pulp
¾ cup fresh carrot juice
1 cup chopped nuts

Preheat oven to 350°. Prepare 2 loaf pans by lining with buttered brown paper and buttering sides of pans. Cream butter with sugars and beat until fluffy. Add eggs and beat well. Mix together dry ingredients and beat into egg mixture. Beat in carrot pulp and carrot juice. Fold in chopped nuts. Pour into prepared pans. Bake for approximately 45 minutes (test for doneness); cool on a rack before removing from pans.

LEMON TEA BREAD

This lemon bread recipe is one of my favorites to have at a tea party. The lemon sauce keeps it moist and gives it a real lemon flavor.

6 tbs. butter
1 cup sugar
2 eggs
½ cup milk
½ lemon, pulp and rind
1½ cups flour

1 tsp. baking powder
¼ tsp. salt
1½ cups chopped nuts
2 lemons, juiced
⅔ cup sugar

Preheat oven to 350°. Prepare a loaf pan by lining with buttered brown paper and buttering sides of pan. Cream butter and sugar together, add eggs and beat well. Add milk and lemon (pulp and rind) and beat well. Slowly beat in flour, baking powder, salt and nuts; mix well. Bake for 50 to 60 minutes until loaf just springs back when touched. While bread is baking, cook juice of 2 lemons and ⅔ cup sugar together until sugar is dissolved. Immediately pour over bread when it is removed from oven and leave in pan until completely cool before removing.

CRANBERRY APPLE MUFFINS

These are wonderfully moist and a great way to use both cranberry and apple pulp.

1 egg
3/4 cup apple juice or milk
3/4 cup apple pulp
1/4 cup butter, melted
13/4 cups flour
1/2 cup sugar
1/2 cup brown sugar

11/2 tsp. baking powder
1/2 tsp. baking soda
1/2 tsp. salt
1 cup cranberry pulp
4 tbs. sugar
1 tsp. cinnamon

Preheat oven to 400°. Combine egg, apple juice, apple pulp and melted butter. In a separate bowl, combine flour, sugar, brown sugar, baking powder, baking soda and salt. Mix egg and flour mixtures together until just moistened. Stir in cranberry pulp. Spoon batter into 12 greased muffin tins. Mix 4 tbs. sugar and cinnamon together and sprinkle over muffins. Bake for 15 to 20 minutes (testing for doneness). Remove from the pan and cool on a rack.

LEMON APPLE OAT MUFFINS

12 muffins

A wonderful high-fiber muffin with a lemon glaze that gives a strong lemon flavor.

1 egg
½ cup apple juice or milk
¼ cup vegetable oil
¼ cup fresh lemon juice
¾ cup oats
1¼ cups flour
½ cup brown sugar
1½ tsp. baking powder
1 tsp. baking soda

1 tsp. cinnamon
½ tsp. nutmeg
½ tsp. salt
1 cup apple pulp
½ cup chopped nuts
¾ cup powdered sugar
1½ tbs. fresh lemon juice
1½ tbs. butter, melted

Preheat oven to 400°. Combine egg with apple juice (or milk), oil and ¼ cup fresh lemon juice. Stir in oats, mixing well. In a separate bowl, combine flour, brown sugar, baking powder, baking soda, cinnamon, nutmeg and salt. Stir in apple pulp and nuts. Mix egg mixture with flour mixture, stirring until just moistened. Spoon into greased muffin tins and bake 15 to 20 minutes.

Mix powdered sugar, 1½ tbs. lemon juice and melted butter together, beating until all lumps are gone. Remove muffins from tins and dip warm muffins into glaze. These muffins are best when served warm.

APPLE BRAN MUFFINS

36 muffins

This is a wonderful way to get your bran! I particularly like this recipe because the batter can be held for several weeks in the refrigerator and used as needed. You can substitute really any fruit pulp in place of the apples to give it a different flavor.

1 cup raisins or chopped dates
1 cup oatmeal
1 cup boiling water
2 eggs, beaten
1 cup sugar
½ cup vegetable oil
2 cups buttermilk
1 tsp. cinnamon

1 tbs. baking soda
½ tsp. salt
1½ cups whole wheat flour
1½ cups flour
2 cups all-bran cereal
1 cup apple pulp
1 cup walnuts, chopped, optional
warmed honey for glaze

Preheat oven to 375°. Mix raisins (or dates), oatmeal and boiling water together and let stand. Combine eggs, sugar, oil and buttermilk and add to oatmeal mixture. Mix together cinnamon, baking soda, salt, flours and all-bran; add to oatmeal mixture. Stir in apples and walnuts if desired. Fill greased muffin tins ¾ full and bake for 15 to 20 minutes. Glaze with a light coat of warmed honey while muffins are still warm.

CINNAMON APPLE MUFFINS

12 muffins

This quick, simple muffin has a crispy cinnamon sugar topping.

1 cup flour
½ cup whole wheat flour
½ cup brown sugar
2 tsp. baking powder
¼ tsp. salt
½ tsp. cinnamon

½ cup fresh apple juice
1 egg, beaten
¼ cup vegetable oil
¾ cup apple pulp
4 tbs. brown sugar
1 tsp. cinnamon

Preheat oven to 400°. Mix flours, brown sugar, baking powder, salt and cinnamon together and set aside. Mix apple juice, egg and oil together; stir into flour mixture. Add apple pulp and stir until just mixed in. Spoon batter into greased muffin tins. Mix brown sugar and cinnamon together and sprinkle over batter in tins. Bake for 15 minutes (or until a knife inserted in the center of a muffin comes out clean). Remove from oven and cool on racks.

CARROT OATMEAL MUFFINS

12 muffins

Carrots add moisture, fiber and flavor to these muffins. But also consider substituting other vegetables in place of the carrots, such as zucchini.

½ cup carrot pulp
¾ cup brown sugar
½ cup vegetable oil
1 egg, beaten
¼ cup carrot juice or water
½ tsp. vanilla
½ cup flour
½ cup whole wheat flour

¾ cup oatmeal
1 tsp. baking powder
¾ tsp. baking soda
¾ tsp. salt
1½ tsp. cinnamon
½ tsp. nutmeg
½ cup chopped nuts, optional

Preheat oven to 400°. Mix carrot pulp, brown sugar, oil, egg, carrot juice and vanilla together. In a separate bowl, mix together flours, oatmeal, baking powder, baking soda, salt, cinnamon, and nutmeg. Mix carrot and flour mixtures together; stir in nuts if desired, stirring just until moistened. Spoon into greased muffin cups and bake for 15 minutes or until muffins spring back to the touch. I like these best served warm.

PINEAPPLE MUFFINS

12 muffins

Pineapple gives breads and muffins a wonderful flavor and moisture. If you use the pulp for baking, you should not juice the pineapple with the skin on.

1¾ cups flour
¾ cup milk
½ cup brown sugar
4 tbs. butter, melted
2 tsp. baking powder
1¼ cups pineapple pulp
½ tsp. salt
½ cup chopped nuts
2 eggs, beaten

Preheat oven to 400°. Combine flour, brown sugar, baking powder and salt. In a separate bowl, combine eggs, milk and butter; stir in pineapple and nuts. Combine flour mixture and pineapple mixture until just moistened. Spoon into greased muffin cups and bake for 15 to 20 minutes.

FRUITED MUFFINS

12 muffins

Almost any muffin recipe can be converted to a high-fiber, fruit muffin by adding fruit pulp and making sure the batter isn't too wet. If it is, simply increase the dry ingredients (including the spices) until you get a slightly thicker batter that won't run off a spoon.

½ cup slivered almonds
¼ cup pineapple pulp
2 eggs, beaten
½ cup brown sugar
¼ cup vegetable oil
1 cup whole wheat flour

1 cup flour
2 tsp. baking powder
¾ tsp. cinnamon
¼ tsp. salt
1 cup apple pulp
¾ cup raisins

Preheat oven to 400°. Grease muffin cups and sprinkle with ½ of the slivered almonds. Combine pineapple pulp, eggs, brown sugar and oil. In a separate bowl, combine flours, baking powder, cinnamon and salt. Combine pineapple mixture with flour mixture and apple pulp. Fold in raisins. Spoon into muffin tins and sprinkle with remaining almonds. Bake for 15 to 20 minutes. Test for doneness.

PEACHY MUFFINS

12 muffins

Here is a great way to use up peach pulp. I like a moist muffin with a crunchy topping.

1½ cups flour
½ cup sugar
2 tsp. baking powder
1 tsp. cinnamon
¼ tsp. salt
½ cup butter, melted
⅓ cup milk

1 egg
1¼ cups peach pulp
1 cup pecans, chopped
⅔ cup brown sugar
½ cup flour
1½ tsp. cinnamon
4 tbs. butter, melted

Preheat oven to 400°. Combine flour, sugar, baking powder, cinnamon and salt. In a separate bowl, combine ½ cup butter, milk, egg and peach pulp. Stir in flour mixture until just moistened. Spoon into greased muffin cups. Combine pecans, ⅔ cup brown sugar, ½ cup flour, 1½ tsp. cinnamon and butter; stir until crumbly. Spoon on top of muffin batter and bake 15 to 20 minutes.

GINGERBREAD APPLE DESSERT

Servings: 8

This is a new twist to gingerbread that adds moisture, a little different texture and that wonderful hint of apples.

3 cups apple pulp
3/4 cup sugar
2 tbs. fresh lemon juice
1 egg
1/4 cup sugar
1/2 cup buttermilk (or sour milk)
1/4 cup molasses
1 cup flour

1/2 tsp. salt
1 tsp. baking soda
1/2 tsp. baking powder
1/2 tsp. nutmeg
3/4 tsp. ginger
1/2 tsp. cinnamon
2 tbs. butter, melted

Preheat oven to 350°. Remove core and juice apples with skin on. Mix apple pulp with sugar and lemon juice and spread in a buttered baking dish. Bake for 10 minutes. Beat egg and sugar together; add buttermilk (or sour milk) and molasses. In a separate bowl, mix flour, salt, baking soda, baking powder, nutmeg, ginger, and cinnamon together. Add this to liquid ingredients. Add melted butter and mix well. Pour over hot apples and bake for an additional 30 minutes. Serve with whipped cream or ice cream.

STEAMED CARROT PUDDING

Servings: 12

Carrot pudding is a moist, steamed pudding similar to Christmas plum pudding. This is a great way to use up several kinds of pulp. I like to top this with a sweet lemon sauce or the traditional hard sauce.

1 cup carrot pulp
1 cup potato pulp
1 cup apple pulp
1/3 cup fresh apple or carrot juice
1 cup sugar
1/2 cup butter
1 cup flour

1/2 tsp. salt
1 tsp. baking soda
1 tsp. cinnamon
1/2 tsp. nutmeg
1/4 tsp. cloves
1/2 cup raisins

Line a pudding steamer pan with waxed paper and grease very generously with butter. Mix all ingredients together with a beater. Depending on moisture of pulp, you may need to increase juice slightly. Mixture should be very thick but not dry looking. Spoon into steamer pan and smooth top. Cover with a layer of buttered waxed paper. Seal and steam for 2 1/2 hours.

Note: If you don't own a pudding steamer pan, either butter a glass Pyrex bowl or line a coffee tin with buttered waxed paper, spoon in the mixture, cover with a layer of buttered waxed paper and then place a piece of aluminum over the top, crimping the edges to seal.

ENTRÉES, SIDE DISHES AND MORE

BRAISED RICE

A nice alternative to plain rice for a meal. It adds color, fiber and more flavor to your starch and is a great way to use leftover pulp.

4 tbs. butter
½ cup celery pulp
½ cup onion pulp
½ cup carrot pulp
1¼ cups rice

1½ cups beef or chicken broth
½ cup white wine
½ cup water
1 bay leaf
salt and pepper to taste

Preheat oven to 350°. In a heavy saucepan with cover, melt butter and add celery, onions and carrots. Cook for 5 minutes on medium heat. Add rice and stir for 2 minutes. Add broth, wine, water, and bay leaf; bring to a boil. Season with salt and pepper and cover. Set in lower third of oven for 25 minutes or until tender.

VEGETABLE WILD RICE STUFFING

Servings: 8

Another way to use vegetable pulp and add color to dark wild rice. Wild rice stuffing is great in cornish hens, chicken or even turkey.

3/4 cup onion pulp
1/2 cup carrot pulp
1/2 cup celery pulp
4 tbs. butter
1 bay leaf
2 cups wild rice
3 1/2 cups chicken stock
1/2 tsp. thyme
salt and pepper to taste

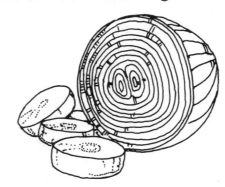

Sauté onion pulp, carrot pulp and celery pulp in butter for about 10 minutes. Add bay leaf, wild rice, chicken stock, thyme and a little salt and pepper. Cover and cook for 30 minutes (check for sticking). Taste and adjust seasonings to your personal taste. Test for doneness. When rice is tender, drain off any excess liquid and fluff with a fork. Cool before stuffing.

AUTUMN RICE PILAF

What makes this pilaf special is the apple juice and raisins. Use it to stuff roast pork, turkey or chicken.

2 cups carrots, diced
1¼ cups butter
2 red apples, diced
2 tbs. fresh lemon juice
¾ cup fresh apple juice
¾ cup water

1 cup rice, raw
½ cup raisins
½ tsp. cinnamon
1 tsp. salt
½ cup walnuts
½ cup green onions, diced

Heat butter and sauté carrots until tender-crisp. Sprinkle apples with lemon juice to prevent discoloration. Mix apple juice with water, bring to a boil and add rice, raisins, cinnamon, and salt. Reduce heat, cover and simmer for 15 minutes. Stir in green onions and walnuts just before serving.

SPINACH RICE

Here is a great way to use leftover spinach from juicing. Spinach juice stimulates and tones the liver, gall bladder, blood and lymph circulation, and large intestine. I like what it does to plain rice, too.

1 cup spinach pulp
2 tbs. butter
3/4 cup onion pulp
1/2 cup celery pulp
1 cup rice, raw

2 cups chicken stock
1/2 tsp. dill weed
1/4 tsp. pepper
1/8 tsp. nutmeg
1 tsp. salt

Melt butter in a large saucepan. Sauté onions in butter until golden; add celery pulp and rice and sauté until browned. Stir in chicken stock, dill weed, pepper, nutmeg and salt. Stir in spinach and bring mixture to a boil; cover and simmer until all liquid is absorbed (about 25 minutes).

ORANGE RICE

Instead of plain rice tonight, consider orange rice. It's great with chicken dishes, baked ham or roast pork.

4 tbs. butter
3/4 cup celery pulp
2 tbs. onion pulp
2 tbs. grated orange peel
2 cups fresh orange juice
2 cups rice, precooked
3/4 tsp. salt
1/4 tsp. thyme

Melt butter in a skillet, add celery and onion pulp and cook until tender. Stir in orange peel and juice; heat. Gently stir in cooked rice and seasonings. Adjust seasonings to personal taste and serve.

ORANGE PRALINE YAMS

Servings: 8-10

This is one of those holiday dishes that makes plain yams into an incredible vegetable dish that you could almost serve for dessert.

2 cans (2½ lb. each) yams, drained or 4 lb. cooked yams or sweet potatoes
⅔ cup fresh orange juice
1 tbs. grated orange rind
5 tbs. brandy, optional
2 tsp. salt
pepper to taste
1 tsp. ginger
4 tbs. butter
⅓ cup brown sugar
3 egg yolks

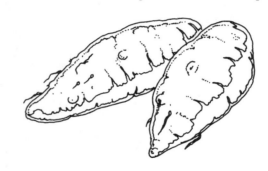

With an electric beater, beat yams or sweet potatoes until smooth. Mix in remaining ingredients, beating until mixture is light and fluffy. Butter a 12-inch shallow casserole. Pour in yam mixture, smoothing top evenly. Prepare topping and spread evenly over yam mixture.

PRALINE TOPPING

1 cup brown sugar
10 tbs. butter, melted
1⅓ cups chopped pecans
1 tsp. cinnamon

Mix all ingredients together in a small bowl. (This is quite sweet, so you may want to adjust sugar to your personal taste). Spread evenly over yam mixture and bake at 350° for 45 minutes or until golden brown and bubbly. Let stand 10 minutes before serving.

ORANGE CARROTS

Servings: 6

If people would learn to dress up vegetables even with simple sauces, I think children (and picky eaters) would like them much better. This is a favorite with my nephews.

1 lb. carrots, sliced
3 tbs. butter
3 tbs. orange marmalade
1 cup dried apricots, chopped
½ cup fresh orange juice
salt and white pepper to taste

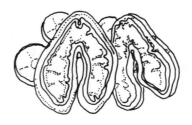

Cook (or steam) carrots until tender crisp. In a saucepan, combine cooked carrots, butter and orange marmalade; set aside. Plump apricots in orange juice in a microwave. Add this to carrots and heat through. Add seasonings and taste.

PAPAYAS WITH FRESH LIME

Servings: 8

This is a unique experience. I had this at a luncheon served with chutney chicken salad. It is a great accompaniment for a meal with a tropical theme.

4 papayas
½ cup butter
¼ cup fresh lime juice
1 tsp. fresh ginger juice
8 tsp. brown sugar

Preheat oven to 350°. Cut papayas in half (lengthwise) and remove seeds. Place in a shallow baking dish filled with about 1 inch of water. In each papaya half, place 1 tbs. butter, ½ tbs. lime juice, ⅛ tsp. ginger juice and 1 tsp. brown sugar. Bake for approximately 30 minutes, covering with foil if papayas begin to brown. Serve warm.

SPINACH SALAD WITH ORANGE DRESSING

Servings: 6

Oranges are a great compliment to spinach and both are packed with vitamins.

1 lb. fresh spinach, torn into pieces
1 lb. prawns or shrimp
1 avocado, peeled and sliced
1 tbs. fresh orange juice
3 oranges, peeled and sectioned
3 green onions, chopped
⅔ cup vegetable oil (I like to blend several kinds)

½ cup fresh orange juice
2 tbs. sugar
1 tbs. red wine vinegar or fresh lemon juice
¼ tsp. salt
¼ tsp. dry mustard
⅛ tsp. Tabasco sauce

Combine spinach, prawns (or shrimp), avocado (which has been combined with 1 tbs. orange juice) and orange sections together in a salad bowl. Using a blender or food processor, combine oil, orange juice, sugar, vinegar (or lemon juice), salt, mustard and Tabasco sauce; blend until homogenized together. Taste and adjust seasonings. Chill. Just before serving sprinkle dressing over spinach salad and serve immediately.

TOMATO MEAT LOAF

Servings: 8

This is a very simple meat loaf that can be different every time if you get creative with alternative vegetable pulps.

1½ lb. ground beef or turkey
¾ cup oatmeal, uncooked
2 eggs, beaten
¼ cup onion pulp
2 tsp. salt
½ tsp. pepper
1 cup fresh tomato juice
optional spices: oregano, basil, thyme, or even poultry seasoning if you are
  using ground turkey

Preheat oven to 350°. Combine all ingedients thoroughly. The seasonings are not necessary, but allow yourself to be creative. I usually fry up a little piece of meat mixture and taste it before baking to adjust seasonings to my personal taste. Pack firmly into a loaf pan and bake for 1 hour. Remove from oven and drain off any excess fat.

CITRUS MEAT BALLS

These meatballs can be used as an appetizer or part of a main meal, ideal served with rice.

1 egg, beaten
2 tbs. flour
½ tsp. salt
⅛ tsp. pepper
1 lb. ground round steak
1 clove garlic, minced
¾ cup vegetable oil (for frying)
1 tsp. salt
1 cup beef or chicken stock
2½ tbs. cornstarch
1 tbs. soy sauce
½ cup fresh lemon juice
½ cup sugar
3 oranges, sectioned
1 green pepper

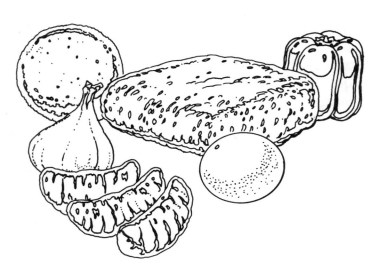

Mix egg, flour, ½ tsp. salt and pepper together. Mix ground beef with garlic and shape into 16 meat balls. Heat oil in a skillet and add 1 tsp. salt. Coat meat balls with egg batter and brown on all sides in hot oil. Pour excess fat from skillet and pour ⅓ cup of beef or chicken stock over meat. Cover and simmer for 10 minutes. Combine cornstarch, soy sauce, lemon juice and sugar with remaining ⅔ cup stock and pour over meat balls. Cut green pepper into 1-inch cubes and boil for several minutes. Remove from heat and rinse with cold water. Add blanched green pepper and orange sections to meat sauce and cook until green peppers and oranges are heated. Serve immediately.

VEGETABLE MEAT LOAF

Servings: 8-10

This is a great way to use leftover vegetable pulp and add fiber and more flavor to your regular meat loaf.

2 lb. ground beef or turkey
½ cup tomato sauce
2 cups bread crumbs
1 tsp. oregano
1 egg, beaten
1 tsp. basil

½ cup onion pulp
1 tsp. minced garlic
½ cup carrot pulp
1 tsp. salt
½ cup green pepper pulp
½ tsp. pepper

Preheat oven to 350°. Mix all ingredients together. Fry a small piece of ground meat mixture and taste in order to adjust seasonings to your personal taste. Press raw meat mixture into a loaf pan and bake for 1 hour. Remove from oven and drain off any excess fat before serving.

NOTE: Always let meat loaf set for 5 to 10 minutes before slicing.

ROLLED STUFFED BEEF

Stuffing is a great way to use vegetable pulp. This is only one example. Consider vegetable stuffings in chicken, pork chops, or even served as a side dish instead of potatoes.

6 cube steaks
4 tbs. butter
3/4 cup onion pulp
1 cup celery pulp
1 1/2 tbs. parsley pulp
1 cup bread crumbs

1/8 tsp. ginger
1/4 tsp. paprika
salt and pepper to taste
1/2 cup flour
1 cup beef stock
1/2 cup red wine

Melt 2 tbs. butter in a skillet, add onion and celery pulp and sauté for several minutes. Add parsley, bread crumbs, ginger, paprika, salt and pepper; stir. Spread stuffing equally on 6 cube steaks and roll up, securing with toothpicks. Dredge steak rolls in flour and brown in the remaining 2 tbs. butter. Place in a baking dish and pour on stock and wine. Bake in 350° oven for one hour.

ENTRÉES, SIDE DISHES AND MORE   155

APPLE PORK CHUTNEY

This is one of my favorite dishes to serve when I'm in a hurry. It goes well with a rice side dish and a light dessert like lemon mousse.

4 pork tenderloins (about 1 lb. each)
½ cup butter
1 large onion, chopped
1 cup apple pulp (I prefer Golden Delicous)

½ cup chutney
1¼ cups cream
1 tsp. Dijon mustard
½ tsp. curry powder
salt and pepper to taste

Cut pork tenderloin into ½-inch slices (medallions). In a large skillet over medium heat, cook medallions in ¼ cup butter (just until there is no pink left), remove and keep warm. Sauté onion in remaining ¼ cup butter until golden. Add apple pulp and cook for approximately 2 minutes longer. Stir in chutney and cream. Cook to reduce cream and thicken mixture. Add mustard, curry, salt and pepper. Return meat to pan, allow meat to heat and serve immediately.

APPLE PORK CHOPS

Servings: 4

This is a quick way to liven up pork chops and use up apple pulp. Always remember that fresh apple juice as well as the pulp will darken very quickly, so use immediately or mix with a little lemon juice to prevent discoloration.

4 pork chops
salt and pepper to taste
1 tbs. oil
1 onion, sliced
2 tbs. butter
1 cup apple pulp
1 cup fresh apple juice
1 tbs. fresh lemon juice (juice with peeling)
¼ tsp. rosemary

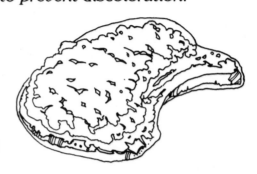

Heat oil in a skillet, season pork chops with salt and pepper and fry until no pink remains (approximately 5 minutes per side). Remove from skillet and keep warm. Sauté onions in skillet in 2 tbs. butter until tender. Add apple pulp and continue cooking for 2 minutes. Add apple juice, lemon juice and rosemary. Cover and cook for 5 minutes. Serve immediately over pork chops.

BAKED BARBECUE RIBS

Servings: 4-6

Every once in awhile I get a craving for ribs. When the ribs are actually cooked in the barbecue sauce, the flavor is really enhanced. This is a great year-round dish because it is baked in the oven.

4 lb. ribs (I prefer country style)
2 qt. water
1 cup mixed vegetable pulp (onion, celery, carrot, etc.)
2 tsp. salt
1 tsp. whole peppercorns
1 tbs. vinegar
1 cup onion pulp
4 tbs. butter

4 tbs. vinegar
6 tbs. Worcestershire sauce
1 tbs. mustard
4 tbs. brown sugar
½ cup fresh lemon juice
28 oz. ketchup
1¼ cups water
1 cup celery pulp
salt to taste

In a large soup kettle, combine ribs, water, mixed vegetable pulp, salt, peppercorns and 1 tbs. vinegar together. Bring to a boil and let simmer for about ½ hour. Remove ribs (discarding remaining ingredients) and place them in a shallow baking dish. In a large saucepan, brown onion pulp in butter for several minutes and add remaining ingredients. Let simmer until slightly thickened. Pour this sauce over ribs and bake at 350° for about 1 hour.

BAKED CHICKEN VEGETABLE WONTONS

This is a great appetizer with an Oriental flare. By varying the types of vegetables and even changing the meats (you can use pork or even ground beef) you can create endless variations.

8 oz. chicken
½ cup carrot pulp
¼ cup celery pulp
1 tbs. soy sauce
1 tbs. sherry

2 tsp. cornstarch
2 tsp. grated ginger root
⅓ cup plum or sweet and sour sauce
24 wonton wrappers (square)
3-4 tbs. butter, melted

Preheat oven to 375°. Grind chicken in a food processor or meat grinder. Fry in a nonstick skillet (adding a little oil if necessary), until just barely cooked. Add carrot pulp, celery pulp, soy sauce, sherry, cornstarch, ginger root and plum sauce. Taste and adjust seasoning. Place a large teaspoon of filling in the center of a wonton, wet all the edges with a little water, carefully bring the opposite points together and pinch. Then pinch along the four side seams to seal well. Brush sides and bottom of filled wonton with melted butter and place on a cookie sheet. Bake for 10 minutes or until browned and crisp.

HAWAIIAN CHICKEN

This is a quick and easy way to prepare chicken and use up your pineapple pulp.

12 pieces chicken (with or without
  the skin)
4-6 tbs. butter, melted
¼ cup brown sugar
2 tbs. cornstarch
¼ cup fresh lemon juice

½ tsp. Worcestershire sauce
2 tbs. chili sauce
1 tbs. soy sauce
⅓ cup ketchup
1¼ cups pineapple pulp

Preheat oven to 350°. Place chicken pieces in a shallow baking pan and brush with melted butter. Combine brown sugar, cornstarch, lemon juice, Worcestershire sauce, chili sauce, and ketchup together; stir in pineapple pulp. Cook over medium heat until thick. Taste and adjust for personal sweetness. Pour over chicken and bake for 1 hour. Test chicken for doneness; bake longer if needed.

NOTE: Remember not to use the skin of the pineapple when juicing if you plan to use the pulp in cooking.

VEGETABLE SHRIMP STUFFED SHELLS

Makes 4 dozen

I'm always looking for appetizer recipes. One day I saw a picture in a magazine that gave me a great idea to use leftover vegetable pulp and pasta together.

1½ cups carrot pulp
1½ cups celery pulp
2 cups grated sharp cheddar cheese
2 cups fresh shrimp
½ cup chopped green onion
1 cup chopped water chestnuts
1 cup mayonnaise
1 tbs. fresh lemon juice
1 tsp. sugar, optional
pepper to taste
1½ lb. large pasta shells
finely chopped parsley for garnish

Combine carrot pulp, celery pulp, cheese, shrimp, green onions and waterchestnuts together. In a separate bowl, combine mayonnaise, lemon juice, sugar (if desired) and pepper. Combine two mixtures together and refrigerate. Boil pasta in boiling salted water, rinse in cold water and drain shells upside down over paper towels until completely dry. Fill pasta shells with shrimp mixture and serve on a platter lined with dry lettuce leaves. This keeps pasta from sliding on the platter. Garnish with a sprinkle of finely chopped parsley.

NOTE: Besides an appetizer, this makes a great salad to serve for a main course at a luncheon. Simply arrange stuffed shells in a star-shape on a salad plate with a spoonful of the filling in the center.

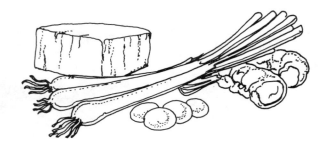

HOT APPLE OATMEAL

Servings: 2

A healthy option to plain oatmeal that has a lot more flavor and fiber!

1 cup fresh apple juice
1 cup water
2 tbs. nonfat dry milk powder
½ tsp. cinnamon
¾ cup oatmeal

½ tsp. grated fresh lemon zest
pinch of nutmeg
pinch of salt
½ cup apple pulp

Combine apple juice, water, dry milk powder and cinnamon. Bring to a boil. Add oatmeal, lemon zest, nutmeg and salt; cook for 8 minutes, stirring occasionally. Remove from heat and add apple pulp. Cover and let stand for 5 minutes.

NOTE: When I use the pulp in cooking I remove the stems and seeds before juicing.

INDEX